The Guide To

BODIE

and
Eastern Sierra Historic Sites

by

George Williams, III

Tree By The River Publishing
Box 935
Dayton, Nevada

The Guide To Bodie and Eastern Sierra Historic Sites
by George Williams III

Published by:
TREE BY THE RIVER PUBLISHING
P.O. Box 935
Dayton, Nevada

1st printing, June, 1981
2nd printing, August, 1981
3rd printing, June, 1982
4th printing, June, 1983
5th printing, June, 1984
6th printing, August, 1984
7th printing, June, 1985
8th printing, July, 1986
9th revised edition, June, 1988

Other non-fiction books by George Williams III:

Rosa May: The Search For A Mining Camp Legend
The Murders At Convict Lake
The Redlight Ladies Of Virginia City, Nevada
Mark Twain: His Adventures At Aurora and Mono Lake
Mark Twain: His Life In Virginia City, Nevada
Mark Twain: Jackass Hill and the Jumping Frog
On The Road With Mark Twain In California and Nevada
The Songwriter's Demo Manual and Success Guide

Library of Congress Cataloging-in-Publication Data

Williams, George, 1949-
        Rhe guide to Bodie and eastern Sierra historic sites.

        Bibliography: p.
        1. Bodie (Calif).—Buildings—Guide-books
2. Historic sites—California—Bodie—Guide-books.
3. Historic sites—Sierra Nevada Mountains (Calif. and
Nev.)—Guide books. 4. Bodie (Calif.)— History.
5. Sierra Nevada Mountains (Calif. and Nev.) —History,
Local. 6. Bodie (Calif.)—Description—Guide-books.
7. Sierra Nevada Mountains (Calif. and Nev.)—Description
and travel—Guide-books. I.Title.
F869.B65W54   1981   979.4'48   81-51267
ISBN 0-935174-03-6   AACR2

Printed in the United States of America

Cover Illustrations by Teri Hill

Author's Introduction to 9th Revised Edition

When I first visited the Eastern Sierra, I was fascinated both by the beauty of the mountains and by the Sierra's rich mining camp history. I had seen plenty of Western boom towns on TV, but I had never visited one in real life, never wandered through their mysterious cemeteries, leaned against their wobbling buildings nor walked their deserted streets where years earlier, men and women made and lived American history.

Bodie, California, thanks to the California State Park Service and a lot of caring people who have worked hard over the years to save and preserve Bodie, is a great opportunity for you to discover what a Western mining town was really like. Once a booming gold, mining town in the 1880's, today Bodie is a California State Park and a National Historic Site. It is just as people left it, currently in a state of arrested-decay. Open all year, you can explore this mining town and its cemetery on your own. During the summer, the Park Service operates tours through the famous Standard Mill.

This guide is divided into three parts: Bodie's history; Bodie's Contemporaries and the Eastern Sierra Business Directory.

The Bodie history presented here is a concise outline designed for the general reader. The history is based on newspaper reports of the day, Mono County Records, Federal Census materials, articles, books and personal interviews with people who lived in Bodie. The history is amplified by rare photos from many sources including the A.A. Forbes Collection, the Burton Frasher, Sr. Collection and from several California and Nevada museums and libraries.

My love and study of Bodie's history began in 1975 when I first visited the ghost town. In the outcast cemetery I discovered the grave of Rosa May, a Bodie prostitute, who had died while saving the lives of stricken miners. For the next three and a half years I researched Rosa May's life in an attempt to discover whether her legend was true. During this time, I found and studied a vast amount of material on Bodie history and had the good fortune to talk with people who had lived in Bodie. My initial research led to my first book, *Rosa May: The Search For A Mining Camp Legend*, the true story of Rosa May's life, which can be ordered through this publisher by using the order form in the back of this book.

They call it "ghost town fever," and I laughed when I first the expression, but it's true. Once you've visited one ghost town the desire to find and explore others gets in your blood. You get hooked. For those of you who like to get out in the boonies and explore these places, this book will help you find other mining towns in the area that were around when Bodie was alive.

Over the years, Bodie has become to me, a good friend and sort of a second home. I visit the town several times each year, sometimes by myself, sometimes with my family, and enjoy camping outside town on BLM land. My wife and I spent part of our honeymoon here while I worked on the Rosa May book. And there were many times when we camped with our infant children in a tent in the hills outside Bodie.

There is a magical quality about Bodie and the Bodie Hills that those who know it come to love. The summers are wonderful with the rich aroma of sagebrush, and the summer thunderstorms that wet the dry earth and leave the sagebrush smelling clean and fresh. And there is something about the altitude, the beauty of the Bodie Hills, the rich blue skies, the clean air, and the night skies with its diamond stars, that cleanses the head and heart. A person tends to think more clearly and hopefully here in the high Sierra.

I love Bodie and I sincerely hope my guide will help you and your family to learn about Bodie and the rich history of the Eastern Sierra. If there's any way I can improve this book, please write me. I'd like to hear from you.

By the way, I am always on the lookout for historic photos of Bodie and other Californa and Nevada mining camps. If you have photos, or know where I may find some, please write me.

Have a good time with my friend, Bodie.

George Williams III,
Camped on Green Creek, Mono County, California
June 1, 1988

I dedicate this book with all my love to my children, Sarah and Michael.

The heart of the prudent getteth knowledge;
and the ear of the wise seeketh knowledge.
Proverbs 18:15

Table of Contents

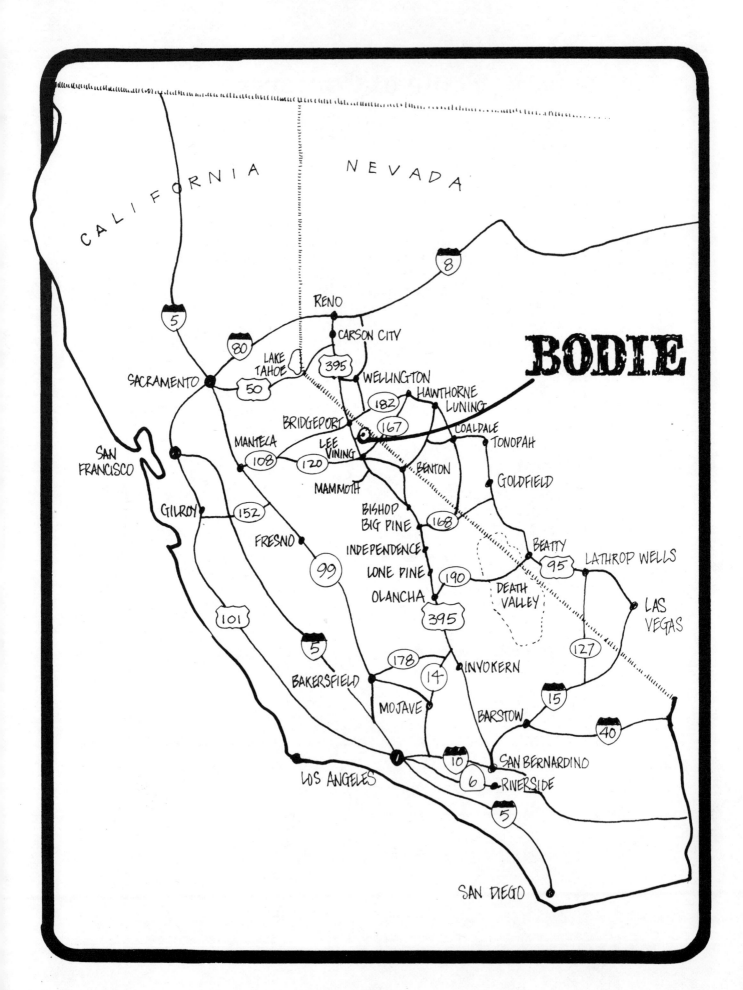

How to Get To Bodie

The map to the left shows the major highway routes from California and Nevada. Once in the Bridgeport or Lee Vining area, there are three roads into Bodie. There is a fourth road from Hwy 167 six miles south of Hawthorne, Nevada.

Easiest Route

If you are in Bridgeport, head 7 miles south. You will see a road sign here pointing the way to Bodie. Ten miles of the 13 mile road to Bodie is paved. There are no service stations or stores in Bodie. Carry plenty of gasoline and food. The trip takes about half an hour.

There is a longer, and more rugged route to Bodie from Bridgeport. This is the Aurora Canyon route. From Bridgeport, take Hwy 182, ½ mile east. On your right you will see the Bridgeport cemetery. Enter the dirt road to the cemetery, then turn right just beyond the cemetery gate. This road leads 15 miles to Bodie.

From Lee Vining

Head North 7 miles to Hwy 167. Take 167, 10 miles east to the Bodie road. This is the Cottonwood Canyon road, a rocky dirt road 10 miles to Bodie.

From Hawthorne

Take Hwy 167 south about six miles. A dirt road on your right (to the west) leads 36 miles to Bodie. The road is well graded but hilly for the first 19 miles. When you enter Bodie Canyon, the road becomes rougher but I made the trip easily in a conventional VW.

Syndicate Mill, Bodie's first major mill built in the 1860's. Ruins are north of Bodie.
Wedertz photo, "Bodie: 1859-1900"

Bodie Area Map

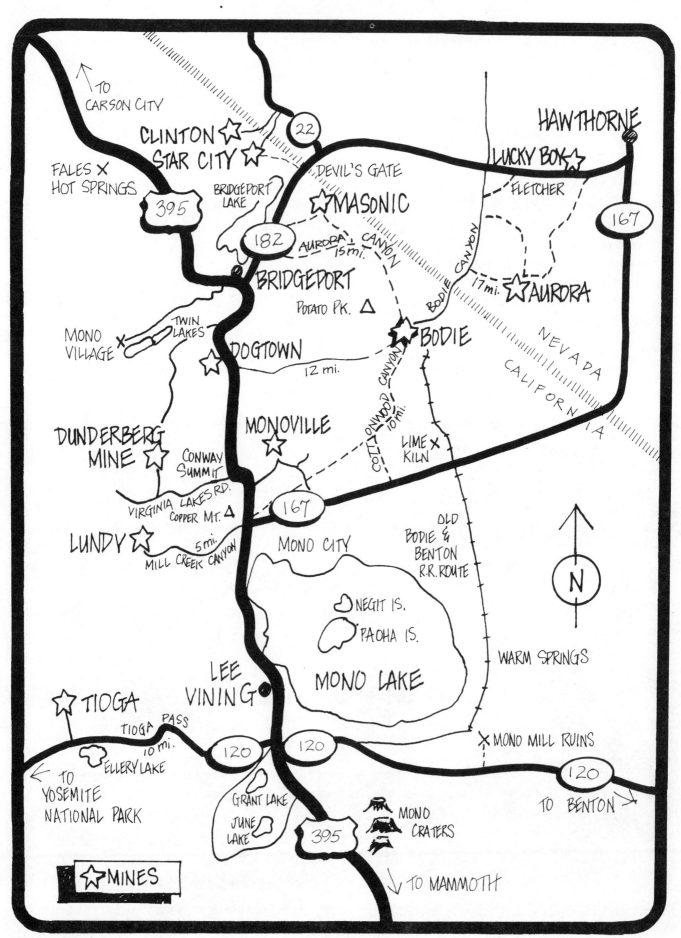

TO CARSON CITY

CLINTON
STAR CITY

FALES ✕
HOT SPRINGS

395

BRIDGEPORT
LAKE

22

DEVIL'S GATE

☆MASONIC

182

AURORA CANYON
15mi.

BRIDGEPORT

Potato Pk. △

HAWTHORNE

LUCKY BOY ☆

FLETCHER

167

☆AURORA

BODIE CANYON

17 mi.

NEVADA

CALIFORNIA

☆ BODIE

MONO
VILLAGE ✕

TWIN
LAKES

☆DOGTOWN

12 mi.

COTTONWOOD CANYON
10 mi.

DUNDERBERG
MINE ☆

MONOVILLE

LIME ✕
KILN

CONWAY
SUMMIT

VIRGINIA LAKES RD.
COPPER MT. △

167

OLD
BODIE &
BENTON
R.R. ROUTE

N

LUNDY ☆

5 mi.

MILL CREEK CANYON

MONO CITY

NEGIT IS.

PAOHA IS.

WARM SPRINGS

MONO LAKE

LEE
VINING

TIOGA ☆

TIOGA PASS
10 mi.

ELLERY LAKE

TO
YOSEMITE
NATIONAL PARK

120

120

✕ MONO MILL RUINS

120

TO BENTON ➤

GRANT LAKE

JUNE
LAKE

395

MONO
CRATERS

☆MINES

TO MAMMOTH

What is Bodie?

Today Bodie is a ghost town, a California state park and a National Historic site. Back in 1879, Bodie was a gold mining boom town. Nearly 10,000 people lived here then. Houses, saloons, hotels and stables covered the narrow valley and hills. There were hundreds of bearded miners in red shirts and tall black boots swinging their lunch buckets as they made their way to and from the mines. There were dapper gamblers dressed neatly in sharp, black suits always on the lookout for a good poker game. There were reckless vagabonds who never worked and spent their days and nights in saloons drinking, looking for quick money or sometimes just looking for trouble. These were the Bodie "Bad Men." Very often they fought each other with fists, knives or guns, shooting and killing each other in the saloons or in the streets.

There were wealthy investors who came to Bodie; blacksmiths and doctors; carpenters and lawyers; saloon keepers, bartenders, card dealers, boiler makers, teamsters and ladies of the evening. They all came to Bodie in droves in 1879 to share in the excitement and hopefully to get their hands on some of the gold that came out of Bodie's mines.

North Bodie in the 1880's. Front row of white buildings face Main Street. Row of small shacks at right of picture behind Main Street saloons were used by prostitutes. Shacks face on Bonanza Street or "Maiden Lane" the Bodie red-light district.
Wedertz photo, "Bodie: 1859-1900"

EASTERN SIERRA MINING HISTORY

1849	Gold discovered at Sutter's Mill near Sacramento. California gold rush begins.
1857	Cord Norst discovers gold at Dogtown. The rush is on.
1859	Monoville — another Norst gold discovery and first major settlement east of the Sierra.
1859	Bodie — gold found by party of four: Bill Bodey, Pat Garraty, Terrence Brodigan and Bill Boyle.
1859	Bill Bodey dies in a blizzard.
1860	Bodie Mining District formed.
1860	Aurora and Masonic — gold discovered during summer.
1864	Benton — Montgomery Mining District formed — Silver.
1865	Benton — highest population in Mono County.
1865	Aurora's boom declines.
1867	Charles Snyder organizes Castle Peak Mining District. Dunderberg mine worked.
1870	Dr. George Munckton buys Dunderberg property.
1875	Mammoth — Gold discovered.
1877	Bodie growing
1878	Tioga — Great Sierra Mining Co. forms Tioga Mining District.
1879	Bodie booms and gold is discovered at Lundy.
1879-81	Bodie at peak; population reaches 10,000.
1882	Bodie mines decline.
1890's	Dunderberg mines show promise.
1895	Cyanide process gives Bodie and Lundy new life.
1902	Masonic re-discovered
1909	Lucky Boy discovery.
1912	Bodie mines decline severely.
1920's, 30's & 40's	Sporadic mining activity in Mono County.

How Did Bodie Come To Be?

In 1849, gold was discovered at Sutter's Mill in the western Sierra foothills about 70 miles southeast of Sacramento. It was this gold discovery that drew men and women from the East and from all parts of the world to California in hopes of getting rich.

Having arrived in San Francisco, there was the usual drinking spree in the many saloons. Afterwards, men sailed up the Sacramento River to Sacramento. There they bought horses, mules and supplies or, if they had no money, simply headed by foot into the Sierra foothills. It was in the foothills that men searched the streams and rivers for placer gold. Placer gold is loose gold; flakes of gold which settle at the edge of creeks and rivers. Placer miners would use a pan to obtain the gold. Having found what they thought was a good spot, they would plop a gob of mud from the stream into their pans. Then they would "wash" the pan by placing the pan in the stream and gently rocking the pan back and forth, allowing the rushing water to sweep away the lighter dirt. Since gold is a heavy metal, the gold would sink to the bottom of the pan and would not be swept away by the water.

Having washed the pan, hopefully there would be left a few flakes of "color". The miners would then carefully scrape the gold into a small leather pouch. This gold was then called "gold dust."

Gold Discovered in Bodie

By 1859, the creeks of the western Sierra foothills had been gone over many times. What gold there was had already been found by earlier placer miners. Men began crossing the Sierra to the eastern foothills. At this time gold was discovered in the area known as Bodie. This is how it happened:

In the fall of 1859, four miners, Bill Bodey, Pat Garraty, Terrence Brodigan and Bill Boyle were camped in what was known as Monoville, near the present town of Mono City on the northwest shore of Mono Lake. (See area map.) The four miners headed into the Bodie Hills. Near what was later to become Aurora, another mining camp, they did some digging, left this site and made their way up Bodie Canyon. It was in Taylor Gulch that they discovered gold. (If you are in Bodie, look east toward Bodie Bluff where the mines are. Running south from Bodie Bluff is Silver Hill. Taylor Gulch is on the backside of Silver Hill.)

It was then autumn in the Bodie Hills and very cold; too cold for unequipped men to stay in the Hills. Soon there would be snow and they would be trapped.

The four miners decided to return to Monoville. They promised each other they would keep their discovery secret. They would return to the site in the spring of 1860.

But Bill Bodey broke his promise. Soon after their return to Monoville, Bodey and another man, "Black" Taylor, returned to the site.

Those who knew Bill Bodey claimed he was about five foot seven. One man claimed Bodey was the dirtiest man he ever met. In any case, Bodey is supposed to have come from Poughkeepsie, New York where he had a tinsmith business. He had a wife and six children and wrote regularly and sent money to support them.

Black Taylor was about four foot nine, a quiet sort of man, dark skinned. His mother was a Cherokee.

Bodey and Taylor built a small cabin at the head of what is today called Green Street in Bodie. This would put their cabin near the Standard Mill. They continued

Early Placer miner working a stream. Los Angeles County Museum.

digging in the area, more now toward Silver Hill.

Tragedy Strikes

In November, Bodey and Taylor made a trip to Monoville for winter supplies. While returning to their cabin, a hard blizzard hit them. Bodey and Taylor struggled to make their way through the snow and cold. Eventually Bodey collapsed. Taylor tried to carry him, but Bodey was too heavy for the small man.

Bodey and Taylor were now about a mile and a half from their cabin, stranded in Cottonwood Canyon. (See area map.) It was then that Taylor decided to return to their cabin, refresh himself and return for Bodey.   He left Bodey wrapped in a blanket.

When Taylor returned to the area where he had left Bodey, the blizzard had thickened. Taylor could hardly make his way through the blinding snow. He was unable to find Bodey and returned to their cabin.

What was left of Bill Bodey was not discovered until spring when the snow melted. Bodey's body had been stripped by hungry coyotes.

Taylor wrapped Bodey's bones in the blanket he had left him in and buried Bodey in a grave about three and a half feet deep. He piled stones on Bodey's grave.

Judge McClinton re-discovered Bill Bodey's grave in 1879. Black Taylor had led him to the grave site years earlier.

Bodie seen from Bodie Bluff, May 18, 1906. Forbes photo.

7

This is what it was like to work in the Bodie mines. Wedertz photo, "Bodie: 1859-1900"

When Bodie boomed in 1879, McClinton felt it only fitting that Bodie's namesake be buried in the camp's cemetery.

McClinton led several men out to Cottonwood Canyon to Bodey's grave. They dug up Bodey's bones and brought them to town where they were put on display for several days. Everyone agreed that Bodey should have a proper burial. Plans were made to have a headstone placed on Bodey's grave. But everyone soon forgot about Bodey with the excitement of gold fever.

Bill Bodey's grave today remains unmarked in the Bodie cemetery. He is believed to be buried in the upper portion of the cemetery, farthest to the west.

Though the camp was named after Bill Bodey, over the years his name was misspelled and the mining camp that became legend came to be known as Bodie.

A Struggling Settlement Becomes A Boom Town

Though gold was discovered in Bodie in 1859, not until 1879 would Bodie actually boom. Several other strikes in the nearby area drew interest away from Bodie.

In 1859, gold and silver were also discovered in Gold Hill and Virginia City, Nevada. There was a great stampede of forty-niners and for the next twenty years Virginia City was the most grand mining camp in the West.

In August of 1860, gold was discovered in Aurora, Nevada, seventeen miles north of Bodie down Bodie Canyon. (See area map.) There was a great rush to Aurora, Mark Twain being among the many gold-thirsty souls. Twain would eventually land a job writing for the Virginia City Territorial Enterprise. He later returned to the East and became a well-known novelist and storyteller often drawing upon his many experiences in the West.

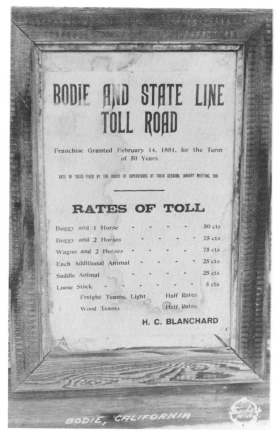

Below, is Blanchard's toll station, located 1 mile north of Bodie in Bodie Canyon. At right, Blanchard's toll rates

9

Bodie stage in early 1900's. Forbes photo.

Because of the excitement of the nearby gold and silver camps, Bodie through the 1860's and early 1870's remained a small camp. There were a few families and a tiny assortment of crude shelters. Various miners continued working the Bodie diggings and mines.

In 1876, a freak cave-in in the Bunker Hill mine (later called the Standard) exposed a rich body of gold ore. The Standard Consolidated Mining Company invested a large sum in lumber and equipment. It was this show of confidence that drew attention to Bodie after nearly twenty years of struggling.

By the fall of 1877, Bodie had grown by leaps and bounds. There were several restaurants, boarding houses, saloons, a grocery store and even a jeweler.

In June of 1878, there was another rich strike, this time in the Bodie Mine. Samples of high grade assayed $1,000 a ton. Within six weeks, the Bodie Mine shipped $1,000,000 in gold bullion!

There had not been a major mining discovery like this in several years. Gold excitement shot through the mining world and the rush was on for Bodie.

By the end of 1878, Bodie had grown into a town of 600 to 800 buildings. The winter of 1878 slowed the influx of travelers but by the spring of 1879, stages could not carry enough gold crazed men and women into Bodie, the new boom town.

Bodie Alive

Perhaps the finest account of Bodie's boom years was written by Grant Smith entitled, "Bodie: The Last Of The Old-Time Mining Camps." Grant Smith arrived in Bodie in 1879 at the age of fourteen and for several years worked there as a telegraph messenger boy. Smith's first-hand account is both interesting and informative. It is presented here in edited form:

Bodie is an unforgettable memory. After more than forty years, it gives me a thrill to speak of it. I went there as a boy of fourteen in June, 1879, when the camp was in its glory, and left in 1881, before the rapid decline had fairly set in; consequently I remember only its golden days...

Bodie was unique; it was the last of the old-time mining camps; the last, in type, of the pioneer days of California. There has been no later camp like it, and never can be, because the old-time Californians who gave Bodie its distinctive atmosphere and charm have nearly all gone where there is no "rainbow chasing." You could no more have another Bodie in these times than you could have another Trojan War with the present-day Greeks as participants. The comparison of the California pioneers with Homer's heroes is not far-fetched. They had much in common...

In order to understand Bodie, one must consider the character of its people and the conditions under which they lived. First, the people:

The leading spirits of the town were "mining camp men" from California and Nevada. I will digress for a few moments to describe the type. The California pioneers were eager, young adventurers from the ends of the earth, mostly Americans. Nearly all of them went to the placer mines first, but only the optimistic, wide-ranging spirits continued to follow min-

ing; the others settled down as farmers, merchants, artisans, and in all other walks of life. The early, shallow placers were soon exhausted, and the miners moved from camp to camp as new discoveries were reported; often leaving good "diggings" to join in the wild rush of a new excitement. Out of these conditions arose a type appropriately called "mining camp men", which included professional men, merchants, and other camp followers. Their ties to a community were not strong, even when they had families, and when a camp began to decline, they eagerly looked about for a fresh field. These men, as a rule, were virile, enthusiastic, and free livers; bound by few rules of conventional society, though with an admirable code of their own: liberal minded, generous to a fault, square dealing, and devoid of pretense and hypocrisy. While the mining camps were not entirely composed of men of this type, it was they who gave the camps their distinctive flavor...

Besides the business and professional men, mine-operators, miners, etc., there were hundreds of saloon-keepers, hundreds of gamblers, hundreds of prostitutes, many Chinese, a considerable number of Mexicans, and an unusual number of what we used to call "Bad men" — desperate, violent characters from everywhere, who lived by gambling, gun-fighting, stage robbing, and other questionable means. The "Bad man from Bodie" was a current phrase of the time throughout the west. In its day, Bodie was more widely known for its lawlessness than for its riches.

Let us now turn to the conditions under which these people lived. Bodie was located in Mono County, fifteen miles east of the Sierra Nevadas, and ten miles north of Mono Lake; in a range of barren, wind-swept hills, entirely devoid of vegetation, save for the ever-present sagebrush. A

Transporting pipe used in the mines and mills. Wedertz photo, "Bodie: 1859-1900"

more uninviting region it would be difficult to imagine. The altitude of the town was 8374 feet; the mines were from five to seven hundred feet higher. The climate was severe, except for some glorious days in midsummer. In winter, cold winds and snow swept it incessantly, and in summer the dust was too often in motion...the winter of 1878-79 was a terrible one...the winter found thousands of people poorly housed, poorly fed, with little employment, and with nothing to do but hang around the saloons and gamble and fight and get drunk and lie out in the snow and die. Hundreds died that winter from exposure and disease, and nearly as many lost their lives by violence. I recall a significant cartoon of the time, showing a man trudging toward Bodie, bearing a tombstone on his back, inscribed somewhat as follows: "John Miner, born Auburn, New York, 1850. Died, Bodie, California,———, 1879."

A Truckee newspaper of that time printed the following prayer of a little girl whose family was about to move to Bodie: "Goodbye God! We are going to Bodie." The editor of a Bodie paper rejoined that the little girl had been misquoted. That what she really said was, "Good, by God! We are going to Bodie."

When I reached Bodie in June 1879, the terrors of the preceding winter had been forgotten, building was going on everywhere, new mines were being opened, new hoisting works erected, new mills being built, the excitement in mining stocks was at its height, nearly everybody had a mine or mining stock that would make him rich, and the region was in a delirium of excitement and activity. Gold and silver coin was as plentiful as nickels nowadays; all of the men about town appeared to have their pockets full of money — and regally they spent it.

Main Street saloons in 1928 before the 1932 fire.   Frasher photo.

...I was the only messenger boy employed in the telegraph office at Bodie during the years of greatest excitement, 1879 and 1880. Necessarily I went almost everywhere to deliver messages. The mines, mills, stores, offices, saloons, gambling houses and the red-light district were visited almost daily... I neither drank nor smoked nor frequented low places. It is gratifying to recall that none of the dissolute persons with whom I came in daily contact ever tried to lead me astray.

All of the conditions in Bodie tended to make men reckless. They were in a remote, barren, sparsely-settled country — "a land that God forgot"; practically without government, and almost without law, which made it a refuge for the lawless; with almost no conveniences of living, poor housing, limited water supply, no sanitary regulations, a harsh climate, forbidding surroundings; no warm, cheerful comfortable places to go except the saloons, the gambling-halls, the dance-

Inside a Bodie saloon in the 1920's. Notice electric lights and spitoon. Frasher photo.

houses, and the red-light district; all leading to drink, to gambling, and to excesses of every kind.

The town was very poorly built up, and remained so; but one or two brick buildings were erected. The saloons and gambling-halls and business houses, up and down the main street, were mere shacks, although sometimes very considerable in size. The boarding houses and lodging houses were of the flimsiest character and poorly heated except in the immediate vicinity of the stove; the homes of the miners and townspeople were built of rough boards, and very small, as a rule. Many people at first lived in tents and dugouts in the hillsides. Heating was difficult and inadequate; toilets were out-of-doors, reached in winter only by a trip through the snow; and the only lights were coal-oil lamps and candles. The only fuel was pinenut wood; knotty and full of pitch and a most excellent fuel. There was no gas, no water except from wells and

Bodie, about 1906. White area is the Standard slum pond. Arrow points to house of Rosa May, Bodie prostitute.

wagons, no coal, no hospitals, no nurses, no churches, no theatres, no entertainments of any sort except such as the people themselves devised.

The traffic in the streets was continuous and enlivening. There were trains of huge, white-topped "prairie-schooners", bringing freight from the railroad, each drawn by twenty or more horses or mules, and pulling one or two large, four-wheeled "trailers"; ore wagons, hauling ore down the canyon to the mills; wood wagons bringing huge loads of pine-nut from long distances, for the mines and mills and for general use; hay wagons, lumber wagons, prospecting outfits, nondescript teams of all descriptions, spanking teams driven by mine superintendents' horses ridden by everybody, and most exciting of all, the daily stages that came tearing into town and went rushing out; the outgoing stages often carrying bars of bullion, guarded by stern, silent men, armed with sawed-off shotguns loaded with buckshot, who did not always succeed in protecting their treasure.

The streets were alive with men at all times of the day and night, and were "wide open." Nearly everybody drank, nearly everybody gambled. Boisterous conviviality was the prevailing spirit. Altogether the street life in Bodie was a sort of continuous motion picture show.

...If there was a town government of any kind in 1879 and 1880, I did not know of it. There were a few deputy sheriffs, appointed by the sheriff who lived at the county seat, twelve miles away; there was also a justice of the peace; but there was practically nothing to hold in check the rough element of the town except the fear of the other fellow's gun or knife. Whiskey was the common drink — beer and wine were too insipid for those tough stomachs — and much whiskey lead to quarreling and gun fighting. Killings were so frequent that the common expression of the day was, "Well, have we got a man for breakfast this morning?" Very often indeed there was more than one dead man. Fortunately, the fighting was almost entirely confined to the rough element, and, so long as they killed off one another, the better citizens did not care. Every once in a while an innocent spectator would get in the way of a bullet, but that was considered partly his own fault for being there.

Cold-blooded murders were uncommon. Most men were killed in open fights, where each side had at least some chance; the victory going to the men quickest in action and surest in aim...

Just off the main street was Chinatown, which was typical, except that it was even more congested and vile than Chinatowns usually are; fronting that, and running down for a considerable distance behind the principal saloons and dance halls, was the red-light district, jocosely called, "Maiden Lane," in which were gathered all types of women from all over the world...

Weapons were oftener drawn than used. Most men that carry guns like to get them out on slight provocation, but they loathe to use them. More than once, I have seen a whole crowd of men with their guns drawn and not a shot fired. Once in a while a man that had killed another would have a hearing before the justice of the peace, but that was as far as the matter went. Bodie had a record of hundreds of men killed by violence, but I recall only two cases of prompt and adequate punishment, in both of which the murderers were taken out of jail by mobs and "hung". One of them was a man who murdered another in cold blood over a woman; the other, the case of an opium-fiend who had been thrown out of a saloon by a bartender, and returned with a shotgun, stood in the doorway, and filled the bartender full of buckshot. Almost invariably these killings occurred at night, in the saloons and gambling halls and in the dance houses, or in the streets outside. I do not know how many men were killed in John Wagner's saloon. That was a typical mining camp saloon, somewhat larger than any of the others. It was a barn-like room, fronting on the main street; probably 30 ft. wide, 100 ft. long, and 15 ft. high. To the left of the swinging doors, as you entered, was the bar, stretched along the side of the room. Opposite the bar, and stretching along in similar fashion was a chop-house, or short-order restaurant, with a long counter and stools in front. The rear of the room was literally filled with gambling tables of one kind and another, principally faro-banks, presided over by silent, watchful dealers, with hundreds, or even thousands, of dollars in gold and silver stacked up in front of them, and a gun always in reach...

It is very easy for men to quarrel when drunk, and much easier to quarrel when drunk and gambling. If there is a woman in the case, so much the worse. There would be hundreds of men every night in John Wagner's saloon. When a shot was fired, the crowd would make a mad rush for the front doors. Many times John Wagner's front doors were carried bodily out into the streets by these stampeded crowds, eager to escape the flying bullets...

John Wagner himself, was a stolid, sober, thrifty, experienced German saloon-keeper, who remained unperturbed during the wildest excitements. His wife, one of the best women that ever lived, was a physician, and devoted her life to ministering to the unfortunate and needy without pay. Her home was just back of the saloon, on a short street that was the outlet of Chinatown and the red-light district — and a fearsome street it was.

While violence was the order of the day, every day, in Bodie, there were no bank robberies, no store robberies, no house-

U.S. Hotel on the east side of Main Street before it burned down in 1932 fire.
Frasher photo.

breaking, and little petty thieving. Property was safer than in San Francisco today. Men's lives were safer too, if they kept away from the resorts known to be dangerous. Of course the bullion stages were frequently held up on the long road to Carson City, usually resulting in the killing of one or more men, but that was expected. The highwaymen always staked their lives in the game, and men spoke of them with respect for their courage...

The camp produced altogether about $21,000,000; of which $14,500,000 was produced by the Standard mine, $4,000,000 by the Bodie, $1,000,000 by the Noonday, and $1,500,000 by all the other mines in the camp. It is an interesting fact that nearly all of the wealth of the Standard and Bodie mines was found within five hundred feet from the surface, and that no ore of importance was produced below eight hundred feet. Within the comparatively small area comprising the Standard and Bodie mines, about one hundred parallel veins were mined for ore, ranging in thickness from a twenty or thirty foot vein of quartz and clay, to seams of high-grade ore less than an inch wide. This mineralized zone, which was extensively mined to a depth of 500 feet, was over 1000 ft. wide and over 3000 ft. long. Much of the ore, particularly that found in the Bodie mine, was extremely rich — so rich, in

fact, that perhaps hundreds of thousands in gold were "high graded" by the miners and others connected with the mine and the mill. (Like Falstaff, the miners have a distaste for the word "steal", when applied to the abstraction of rich gold ore belonging to others, so they coined the milder term "high grade" to express the same thought.) The richest ore from the Bodie mine did not pulverize readily in the mill, because the gold and silver would pound up into massive sheets under the stamps, and had to be shoveled out of the mortar-boxes in order that the stamps could do their duty. All of the gold in the district was heavily alloyed with silver, and was rarely worth more than $12 per ounce. In some of the shallow placer diggings, at the south end of the ridge, the gold was worth only from $3 to $8 per ounce.

A kindly foreman took me down into the Bodie mine to see the "1879 bonanza", and I shall never forget one small drift, or tunnel, that glittered on all sides with gold and silver like the treasure house of Croesus. Illustrative of the liberality of the times is the fact that hundreds of men and women were allowed to visit the Bodie mine when that ore was being extracted, and that the visitors were permitted and even encouraged, to carry away valuable specimens. Visiting the Bodie

Johl's and Donnely's City Market, Occidental Hotel with bay windows.
Frasher photo.

mine became very popular in those days...

In round numbers, the camp produced $21,000,000 in gold and silver, and paid dividends amounting to $7,000,000. The total assessments levied by the various mining companies totaled about $5,000,000; in addition to which perhaps $500,000 was expended on other mines by individuals; so that the total amount of money that was paid in by the stockholders and owners nearly equaled the dividends paid. The camp should be termed a financial success, however, because the gold and silver produced went into the channels of trade and had a very stimulating and beneficial effect throughout the Pacific Coast.

The Gray Mill battery.

The Gray Mill in Bodie Canyon.

Everybody gambled in stocks, which kept the excitment of the community at a high pitch. There were over thirty large mining properties in Bodie whose stocks ere dealt in every day on the San Francisco Stock Exchange. The quotations came every day by telegraph. The phrase that one heard of oftenest in Bodie was "Let's take a drink." The next most popular expression was the inquiry, "How are stocks today?" With few exceptions, those mines were failures, but in 1879-1880, it was confidently expected that every one of them would prove a "bonanza." Stocks moved up and down with startling rapidity. Men were rich today and poor tomorow, and then rich again... Nearly everybody in Bodie, at one time or another, had a good deal of money, but almost everybody left the camp "broke" when "the bottom dropped out."

The curse of Bodie, as it was of "The Comstock," was the stock market, which was manipulated by stock gamblers in San Francisco for their own profit, regardless of the merits of the mines, and without

thought for the thousands that found their ruin in the unholy game...

The people of Bodie were extremely social, but there was no "society life." Living conditions were too hard for that. Social distinctions were lightly drawn, particularly among the men, who themselves came from every grade of society, from the highest to the lowest. Every prominent old-time mining camp contained a large number of well-educated people, both men and women. Even the small, remote places had their quota. That life seemed to hold a peculiar fascination for cultured people of the romantic type. One could always find his level in a mining camp, whatever it was...

The sensational side of life in Bodie is the most interesting, and I have dwelt upon that, but there was another strongly contrasting life — that of the good women of the town. Most of the men that went to Bodie were single, but there were more wives and children than one would expect to find in such a place. These women, as a rule, had lived in other mining camps,

First Standard Mill before it burned down in 1899. Notice piles of cord wood to the right used to power the mill. Wedertz photo, "Bodie: 1859-1900"

and many of them, like their husbands, were of superior type. They, too, were notable for their breadth of view, warm-heartedness, sociability, and for their good works. In the midst of all that tumult and recklessness, they lived quiet, un-eventful and thoroughly good lives. It would be difficult to find a finer type than those old-time mining camp women. Not a few of them had been friends in earlier days, and conditions in Bodie threw them closer together than ever before. They devised practically all of the social enter-tainments of the camp. It was remarkable

how much they did in the way of getting up theatrical performances, dances, sup-pers, Sunday School picnics, sleighing parties, and other diversions. Amuse-ments were few and simple, and all the more enjoyed. A very close relationship grew among those women, just as it did among the men.

One of the remarkable things about Bodie; in fact, one of the striking social features among all mining camps in the West, was the respect shown by even the worst characters to the decent women and the children . Some of the best families in

New Standard Mill built in 1899. Frasher photo.

Ore wagon used to haul ore to mills.

Pouring gold bullion in the Standard Mill about 1900. Notice floor of steel plates.

town lived in the immediate neighborhood of Chinatown and the red-light district, and the women and children could not move out of their houses without passing saloons and all sorts of terrible places. Yet I do not recall ever hearing of a respectable woman or young girl being in any manner insulted or even accosted by the hundreds of dissolute characters that were everywhere. In part, this was due to the respect that depravity pays to decency; in part, to the knowledge that sudden death would follow any other course.

Mining camp life had a very unfavorable effect upon the boys as they grew toward manhood, the example set by their elders could not have been much worse, and the doors of every kind of dissipation were wide open. The good women and the girls, on the other hand, lived their lives apart, respected and even revered. I recall with deep satisfaction the sweet, modest girls with whom I went to school in mining camps.

Nothing draws people together like hardships and a feeling of mutual dependence. Where they are forced to rely upon one another for all their pleasures, and when they are even more dependent in times of sickness and sorrow, a relationship is created such as city people never know.

Living conditions in Bodie were crude and primitive to the last degree, but, oh,

the kindly feeling, the helpfulness, the good fellowship! People were drawn together as I have never seen them anywhere else. A friend in Bodie was a friend for life.

The town was small, congested, and "wide open"; people lived and did as they pleased without pretense; the lives of all were open, and known to men, women and children. Everybody knew what women the different men about town were living with, and all discussed eagerly the sensational news of the day. That gossip was one of the features of the life. Yet people were generous in their judgements; liberal allowances were always made. The absence of meanness, pettiness, and narrowness was one of the striking manifestations of the mining camp spirit.

It has always seemed to me that one

Standard Cyanide plant built in 1895 used to rework tailings. A.A. Forbes photo.

learned more about human nature in a mining camp in a few years than could be acquired in a city in a lifetime. There one saw the human animal in the raw; living boldly, without pretense and without shame — and yet admirable, on the whole. Taking them for all in all, their virtues outweighted their vices. Their sins were mostly against themselves; their better natures showed in their attitude toward others. Somehow, all of the people — even those without the pale of mining camp respectability — showed some admirable traits. Ordinary men became transformed in that atmosphere, taking upon themselves, for the time at least, some of the qualities of the greater spirits...

Bodie Fire House.

Fourth of July in Bodie. Bodie citizens were very patriotic and looked forward to the 4th of July parades, foot races and various contests. A group of citizens is shown here in front of Salisbury store and Temple Saloon. Forbes photo.

24

Bodie schoolhouse. Frasher photo.

Theodore Hoover's house during the early 1900's.
Frasher photo.

James Cain home, Bodie banker and businessman. Now a ranger's residence.
Frasher photo.

Left to right. Dechambeau Building, Odd Fellows Hall, Miner's Union, and Undertaker. Frasher photo.

Inside Miner's Union Hall, now Bodie Museum. Dances and other Community functions took place here. Frasher photo.

Bodie Ghosts

"Within a fortnight two men have been severely beaten over the head with six shooters, one has been shot, one stabbed to death, one man and one woman have been knifed and one woman's skull crushed and she may die tonight," a Bodie newspaperman wrote. Violence took the lives of many men and women in saloons, dance halls and bordellos. Many of Bodie's "Bad Men" found their ticket to the hereafter in a lead bullet.

Take Red Rowe, a reckless, desperate character. Recently released from the Bridgeport jail where he had served time for beating a woman, his typical crime, Rowe strutted up to a Bodie bartender and called for a "cocktail of lava, lighting, bitters and gin and got it!" Red Rowe was finally murdered in 1886 by Andrew Peterson.

Rattlesnake Dick, a tough hombre forever threatening others, was finally taken seriously and shot. Thomas Travis merrily danced the evening away at the Opera House Dance Hall until Tom Dillon, a crazed opium addict murdered him.

Gun fights were common. Jack Braslin was killed in a gunfight, John Kehoe, killed in a gunfight, James Harrington, Charles Slade and countless others, all killed in Bodie gunfights and buried in boothill.

The deaths of these "Bad Men" did not upset the upstanding portion of the community. But the killings of good men outraged them. The murder of Florentine Herriera, a hard working Mexican peddler who was robbed and beaten to death, sickened the community. But it was the cold blooded murder of Thomas Treloar, a miner, that spirited the formation of the Bodie 601, a vigilante group.

The Treloar murder occurred at 1:30 A.M. January 14, 1881. Thomas Treloar and his wife had gone to a community dance at the Miners Union Hall. Joseph DeRoche had made advances toward Treloar's wife which she had refused. As

Bodie jail at the edge of Chinatown. Frasher photo.

Thomas Treloar left the dance, DeRoche waiting in the shadows, leapt out and shot Treloar point blank. Treloar was killed instantly. DeRoche escaped, was caught, escaped again, was caught and finally jailed.

The Treloar murder organized the fear and frustration of Bodie into an impatient—ready for justice—group of men: the Bodie 601.

Forty-eight hours after the Treloar murder, 200 armed men silently made their way through the night to the Bodie jail. Their leader knocked on the jail door. Jailer Kirgan opened up, "All right boys," he conceded, "wait a minute, give me a little time." Four men entered the jail.

Minutes passed. The mob grew impatient. "Bring him out,—open the door—hurry up," they shouted. DeRoche finally emerged. By the horrified look on his face, DeRoche knew what was to befall him.

The mob led DeRoche to the exact spot where he had murdered Treloar. A wooden gallows was moved to the place. DeRoche's coat was removed, a noose was hung around his neck. "Anything to say?" someone asked. "No, nothing," DeRoche said. He was asked again, "I have nothing to say only, Oh God—" "Pull him," someone commanded. The rope ripped tight. DeRoche went up 3 feet, his body twitched for an instant. Within moments he was dead. DeRoche was left hanging and a

Bodie Cemetery. Frasher photo.

This hearse carried many a soul to his eternal rest in Bodie's Cemetery. Frasher photo.

note was pinned to his breast. "All others take warning. Let no one cut him down. Bodie 601."

This was mining camp justice. DeRoche, like other Bodie outlaws is buried in Bodie's outcast cemetery on the lower slope of cemetery hill.

Like other mining camps, Bodie had its share of oddballs. Mike McGowan, the Man Eater, was one. He was booted out of Virginia City for biting off noses and ears during fights. As soon as McGowan landed in Bodie, he tried to chew on Sheriff Taylor's leg. Judge Peterson took aside the "gentle creature who relishes men's noses, ears, thumbs and calves." Mike was requested to leave Bodie which he did.

The saddest Bodie stories are among the women who followed the mining camps, the "demimonde", "ladies of the evening,"— the prostitutes. Prostitutes were as much a part of mining camp life as picks and shovels. Their ends were often very sad.

Eleanor Dumont was one. A pretty, petite French girl, she first showed up in Nevada City in 1855. At that time she was a young, pretty gambler. Women gamblers were a rare thing in a saloon. Men were awed by Dumont's beauty, her quiet confidence and her ability. All treated her with respect.

For the next twenty-four years, Dumont followed the mining camps, to Idaho, to the Black Hills, to Deadwood. At times she lost heavily and turned to prostitution to earn money for gambling. With age, a thin line of dark facial hair emerged above her lip. She was dubbed "Madame Moustache", a name she resented but never shook.

In September, 1879, Dumont was in Bodie. Having lost $300 which she had

A typical Bodie grave encircled by a weathered picket fence.

borrowed, Dumont secretly left Bodie on foot. Two miles south of town she swallowed poison and killed herself.

The famous Eleanor Dumont, alias "Madame Moustache", is buried in the outcast cemetery in an unmarked grave.

Many children are burried in the Bodie cemetery.

French Joe is another sad story. A Bonanza Street prostitute, she was arrested in 1879 for kicking the windows out of a dance hall. A hard drinker, when drunk she became uncontrollably violent. Like Dumont, French Joe left Bodie on foot in 1880. In 1881, remains of her body were found four miles from Bodie near Rough Creek.

Nellie Monroe, a prostitute known in all the mining camps, at 45, an alcoholic and an opium addict, she killed herself in a Bodie hotel.

Emma Goldsmith, another Bodie prostitute who had come from Carson and Virginia City, lived in a small white house behind the bank on King Street, Goldsmith killed herself August 18, 1900. She had paid the Stuart family to take care of her child.

Rosa May, a pretty Irish prostitute, had worked the brothels of Carson and Virginia City for many years before coming to Bodie in the early 1890's. Big hearted and generous, she gave dimes to children for candy. She died in 1912 while nursing miners in a pneumonia epidemic. In spite of her sacrifice, Rosa May was not allowed burial within the cemetery fence and was buried in the outcast cemetery. The author located her hidden grave and restored the fence which had once encircled her grave.

There were other Bodie prostitutes and their lives were tough: Kate Wise had her face beaten to a bloody pulp by Jack Perry. Sailor Jack was beaten by Pat Shea with his lunch bucket. Louis Dunbar was beaten by James McCarthy. Mrs. Jobe Draper was beaten to death by her husband with a black snake whip. Others were Maude Bennets, Daisy Lawrence, Martha Camp, Annie Frank, Agnes Carter, Rosa Olaque, Lottie Johl — and more — nameless women who no doubt died sad, lonely deaths.

Grave of Rosa May, Bodie prostitute. The grave fence was later destroyed by vandals. Frasher photo.

Rosa May in 1879. She was twenty-four.

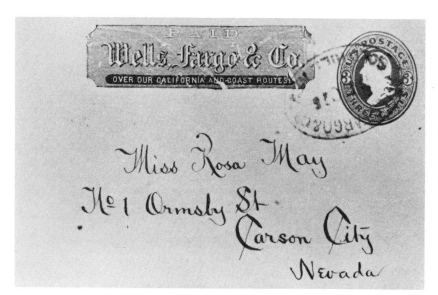

Author replacing Rosa May's fence after her hidden grave was found.

Arrow points to Rosa May's house in north Bodie. Men hauling cyanide plant equipment in foreground. Photo Bodie Park.

Arrow points to Ernest Marks' saloon. Marks was Rosa May's lover. Frasher photo.

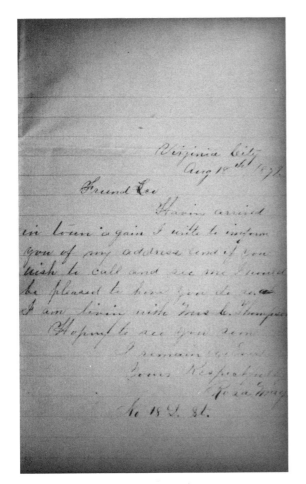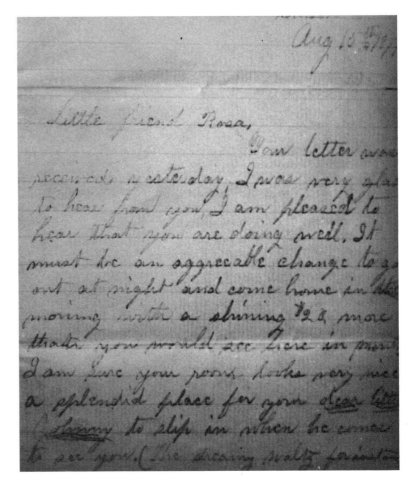

Left, handwriting of Rosa May. Right, letter from Emma Goldsmith to Rosa May. Emma mentions that Rosa May had made $20 in one night, a miner's weeks wages.

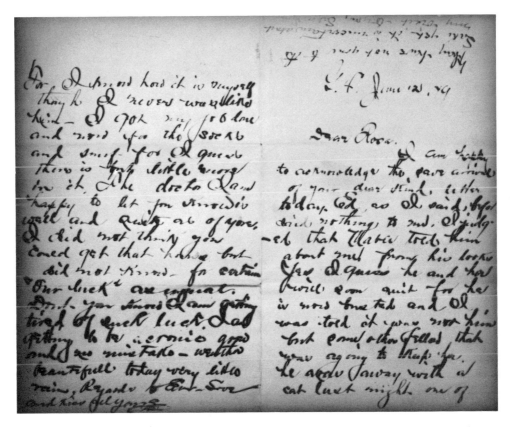

Ernest Marks' letter to Rosa May written in Gold Hill. During late 1870's both Rosa May and Marks lived in Virgina City.

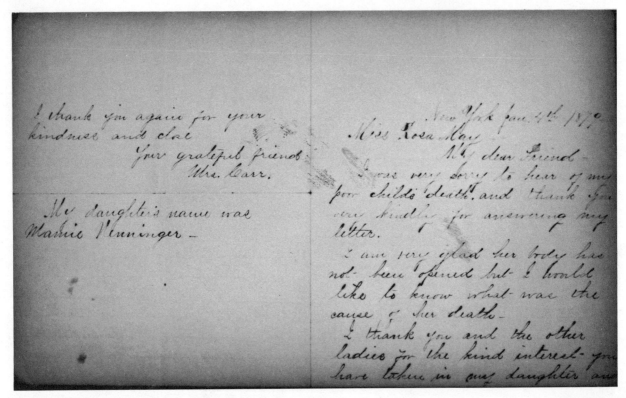

Letter from a Mrs. Carr dated January 4, 1879, written to Rosa May while she lived in Virginia City, Nevada. Mrs. Carr was requesting information about her daughter's strange death. Her daughter had evidently been a fellow prostitute.

Lottie Johl's grave. It is rumored that Lottie worked for Rosa May. Lottie married Eli Johl, a Bodie butcher. In spite of her marriage, Bodie townspeople hesitantly allowed her burial within the fence. Grave can be found at far southwest end of cemetery. Lottie died of poisoning, Nov. 7, 1899. Frasher photo.

Where Did The People Go?

Bodie went the way of all boom camps. Her days of glory were brief, from 1879-82. In 1882 only six mines were operating. Miners lost their jobs and moved on to other camps. Construction of new buildings stopped; carpenters moved on. Houses and properties were put up for sale, businesses left town. The excitement gold had caused was gone.

Yet Bodie managed to stay alive for quite some time. Through the 1880's her population averaged from 1,500 to 2,000. Gradually the mines slowed down and people left town. By the 1890's, Bodie's population had dwindled to 700 — 1,000.

During the 1890's Jim Cain, a Bodie banker and businessman, introduced the cyanide process into Bodie mining. The

Canostoga wagon used by many families when they left bodie

A lonely Bodie ruin as evening nears.

cyanide process was a new way of extracting gold from tailings.

The cyanide process helped keep Bodie alive as late as 1914. With World War I, all mining came to a halt in Bodie but resumed after the war. Various mining companies leased and worked the Bodie mines as late as the 1950's but there were no more new strikes and leasors reaped only minor profits from the old tailings. There was no work in Bodie and little by little people left the camp. Bodie was becoming a ghost town

When people were leaving Bodie, there were no moving companies in the area. People simply packed what they could on one wagon or truck and left the rest behind. That is why many of Bodie's buildings still contain belongings that were left here years ago.

Land Office, formerly Solderling's Assay Office. Frasher photo.

Jim Cain's bank on the left. Frasher photo.

The Bodie fire of 1932 wiped out seventy percent of the town. Frasher photo.

"Bodie Bill", the young boy who started the 1932 fire behind the Sawdust Corner Saloon.

Man hauling water in buckets to fight the fire after Bodie fire hydrants failed. Frasher photo.

Before the fire looking north down Main Street. Frasher photo.

After the fire looking south up Main Street. Second structure on right is what was left of the Bodie bank safe. Frasher photo.

Things To Do In And Around Bodie

In Bodie

1. Use the map included in this book to tour Bodie.
2. Visit the Bodie Museum.
3. Visit the Bodie Cemetery. Search for the oldest grave. Find Rosa May's real grave. Visit Lottie Johl's grave.
4. Picnic at the picnic area just north of town. There is a spring there with cold, sweet Bodie spring water.
5. Hike or camp in the Bodie Hills.
6. Look for Bill Bodey's original gravesite in Cottowood Canyon. (See map.)
7. Drive to Aurora, 17 miles north of Bodie, where Mark Twain prospected and mined. Visit the Aurora Cemetery.
8. Drive to Masonic (See Map.)
9. Climb Potato Peak.
10 Take a different road back to Highway 395.
11 Take Bodie Canyon Road to Hawthrone, Nevada. There's fishing at Walker Lake and gambling at the casinos.
12 Visit Dogtown near the Bodie Road on Highway 395 south of Bridgeport.

Near Lee Vining and Mono Lake

1. See Kit Carson's daughter's grave behind the Mono Inn on 395.
2. Visit Lundy, once a gold mining camp in Mill Creek Canyon.
3. Picnic at the Mono Lake campground.
4. In Lee Vining, visit the Mono Lake Committee. Help save Mono Lake!
5. Visit the Mono Mills site, where lumber was cut for Bodie. (See map.)
6. Visit Obsidian Dome, a mountain of obsidian south of Lee Vining.
7. Visit Yosemite National Park.
8. Go rock hunting.
9. Visit the Tufa Reserve at Navy Beach on the west shore of Mono Lake.
10 Collect brine shrimp at Mono Lake.
11 Retrace the old Bodie railroad route from Mono Mills around the east shore of Mono Lake. Four-wheel drive vehicles only!
12 Visit the Mono Craters, southeast of Lee Vining.

Near Bridgeport

1. Visit Mono County Museum.
2. Fish Bridgeport Lake, East Walker River, Twin Lakes, Virginia Lakes and many fine streams.
3. Visit Travertine Hot Spring, Big Hot and Buckeye Hot Spring. See the author's, *Hot Springs of the Eastern Sierra*.
4. Fales Hot Spring 16 miles north of Bridgeport.
5. Camp at many campgrounds in the area.
6. Annual 4th of July Celebration. Lots of fun!

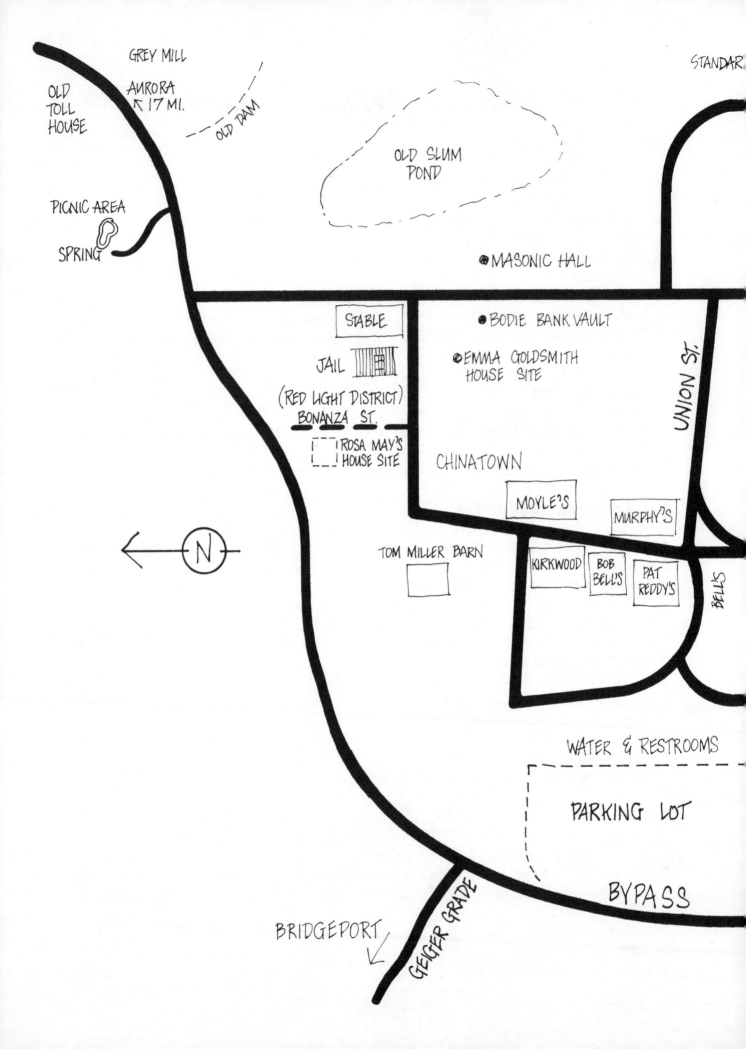

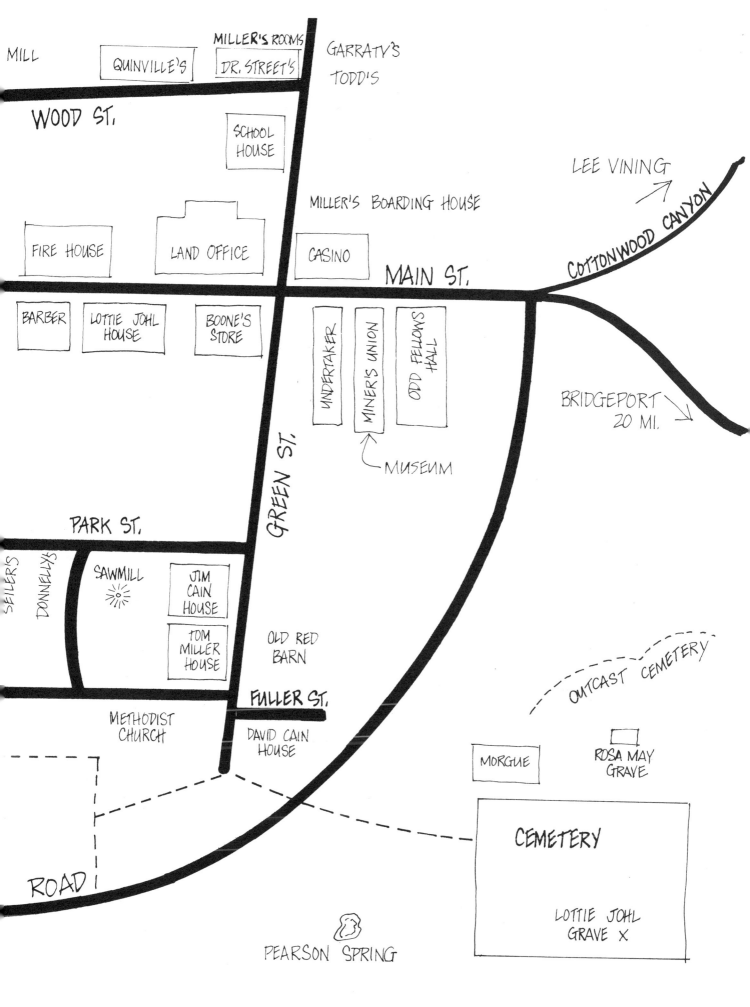

MILL

QUINVILLE'S   MILLER'S ROOMS
              DR. STREET'S   GARRATY'S
                             TODD'S

WOOD ST.

SCHOOL HOUSE

LEE VINING

COTTONWOOD CANYON

MILLER'S BOARDING HOUSE

FIRE HOUSE   LAND OFFICE   CASINO   MAIN ST.

BRIDGEPORT 20 MI.

BARBER   LOTTIE JOHL HOUSE   BOONE'S STORE   UNDERTAKER   MINER'S UNION   ODD FELLOWS HALL

GREEN ST.

MUSEUM

PARK ST.

SEILER'S   DONNELLY'S   SAWMILL   JIM CAIN HOUSE   TOM MILLER HOUSE   OLD RED BARN

FULLER ST.

OUTCAST CEMETERY

METHODIST CHURCH   DAVID CAIN HOUSE

MORGUE   ROSA MAY GRAVE

ROAD

CEMETERY

PEARSON SPRING

LOTTIE JOHL GRAVE X

Bodie's Contemporaries

Aurora, Nevada

Aurora is located 17 miles northeast of Bodie, 3 miles within the Nevada border. Aurora was first thought to be in California until an 1863 survey proved the camp to be in Nevada.

Consulting the area map, you will notice that there are two routes to Aurora. If you are in Bodie, head north around the town and down Bodie Canyon. You will pass the ruins of the Syndicate Mill on your right and farther down the remains of the Sunshine toll house. Bodie Creek will emerge several miles down the canyon and is a source of fresh water. The road to Aurora is 17 miles, rough, but I made the trip in a VW easily. Thirteen miles out you will reach a sandy flats. The road will fork. Go to your right (to the east) 4 miles to Aurora. You will come to the Aurora cemetery about ½ mile from the Aurora ruins. A sign points the way to the cemetery.

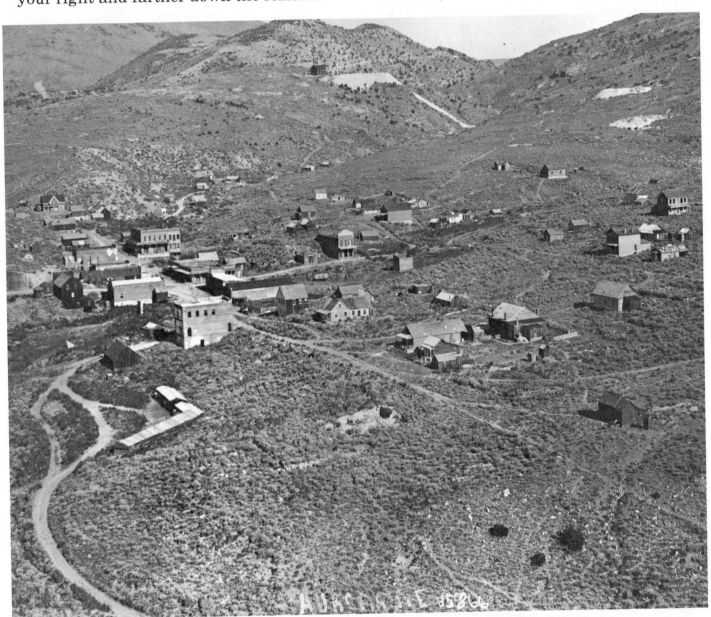

Aurora at the turn of the century. Forbes photo.

Mark Twain's cabin, later hauled to Reno. Forbes photo.

If you are coming from Hawthorne, Nevada, take 167 south about six miles. A dirt road on your right (to the west) leads 19 miles to Aurora. The road is very well graded but hilly.

On August 25, 1860, Jim Corey, Jim Braley and E. R. Hicks, discovered gold in Aurora. Corey and Braley were from San Jose. They had met Hicks, part Cherokee, in Virginia City, Nevada. The three had been camped in the Aurora area when Hicks, while hunting, broke off pieces of a quartz outcropping and found gold. This became the Winnemucca Lode located near the west crest of Esmeralda Hill. The same afternoon, Corey located the Esmeralda Lode and two other claims, the Cape and the Plata. Corey, being well read, named their discovery site Aurora, meaning "Goddess of Dawn." He called the district Esmeralda, Spanish for emerald, because of the beautiful green of the pinon pines in the area.

Within two months of the discovery, prospectors made 357 claims. Corey and Braley shortly sold out for $30,000 each and settled in Santa Clara. Hicks sold out for $10,000 and returned to Arkansas.

In April, 1861, the California legislature passed a bill forming Mono County making Aurora county seat. An 1863 survey would later place Aurora in Nevada. Mono County seat was moved to Bodie and then to Bridgeport.

In April, 1861, the first stage from Carson City arrived in Aurora. The fare was $20 for the 90 mile trip which took 24 hours. Because Aurora was so far from a major supply point, food was high. Meals went for 75¢, $10 a week. Cost of feeding a horse was $3 a day. Gull eggs from Mono Lake were much appreciated and went for 75¢ a dozen.

Early milling of ore was done by the arrastre method, first used by the Mexicans. It was a primitive form of milling

43

done by horses or mules dragging rocks over a circular pit of ore. In June of 1861, the first amalgamating mill was built.

The Esmeralda Star newspaper began publishing May 17, 1862. By August, Aurora's population had reached 3,000 and the camp boasted 22 saloons.

By April, 1863, stages were bringing in 25-30 newcomers a day. Lots were going for $2,500 — 5,000 each. The camp's population had reached 4,000, 200 of which were women and a school was built for the 80 children. There were 761 houses; 64 of them brick, 22 saloons, 2 churches, Masonic and Odd Fellow organizations. Population eventually peaked at 6,000 — 10,000. Sixteen mills were built with a total of 200 stamps crushing ore. The largest mills were the Real Del Monte, built at a cost of $250,000, and the Antelope Mill. Both were huge brick structures in the Gothic style. The Real Del Monte had a battery of 30 stamps and 36 wheeler pans. The foundation of the Del Monte Mill can still be found on Bodie Creek. The Antelope Mill had fewer stamps and pans. Both mills were powered by steam.

Aurora's first excitement slowed in 1865. Several factors contributed to the camp's failure: The original veins were shallow and were exhausted at a depth of 94 feet. The mines were greatly mismanaged. Expensive mills were often idle and did not successfully extract rich metals. Water in the mines was also a real problem. When springs were tapped, the water could not be pumped out fast enough. Stocks were also greatly over-valued. By 1865, half the town had moved on though surface bonanzas had yielded 24 million.

Aurora saloons in 1920's. Frasher photo.

In the early 1870's an English company bought all the Aurora properties but the company went bankrupt.

With the Bodie excitement in the late 1870's, the Aurora mines were reworked and did well until 1882 when Bodie declined.

In 1883 Aurora lost the county seat to Hawthorne and in 1897 the Aurora post office was closed.

Still, Aurora rose again in the early 1900's. The Cain Consolidated Mining Company, owned by Jim Cain of Bodie, purchased the important mines. Cain operted a small mill in Aurora and leased claims he was not working. In 1912, the Jesses Knight interests bought the Cain properties and formed the Aurora Mining Company.

Knight erected a cyanide plant and a 40 stamp mill with a 500 ton per day capacity ty. Shops, warehouses, cottages and bunkhouses were also built. The new construction was over the hill from the old town of Aurora and was called Mangum after one of the owners. Liquor was not allowed in the camp.

The Esmeralda Hotel, like all Aurora brick structures, was dismantled after WWII. Frasher photo.

These new developments caused a rush to Aurora. Old buildings were renovated and new ones built. Because of "dry" Mangum, many new saloons opened in Aurora. These included: The Hermitage Bar, Tunnel Saloon, Aurora Club, Northern, Elite Bar and the First and Last Chance Saloon.

In 1914, Jesse Knight sold the Aurora properties to the Goldfield Consolidated Mining Company. Goldfield completed construction of the cyanide plant and cottages and worked the mines until operations shut down in 1917. The mill, plant and buildings were dismantled and sold. Foundation of the Mangum mill can still be found today.

By 1920, Aurora had only a few residents. The town was eventually deserted and stripped. Brick buildings were torn down and hauled away. Foundations, cemetery and mine sites are left.

A final note: Aurora had some influence on the literary development of one of America's finest authors: Mark Twain, real name, Samuel Langhorn Clemens. Clemens came West as a young man with his brother, Orion. Clemens and Bob Howland, nephew of Nevada Governor Nye, drifted to Aurora in 1862. For a time, Clemens held a major interest in the Wide West mine and would have become wealthy had he and his partners not lost the claim by failing to work it. Clemens ended up doing manual labor in an Aurora mill, tough work which he had no use for.

Virginia City's Territorial Enterprise, was at this time one of the West's top newspapers. Each week Clemens wrote a humorous story, signed it "Josh" and mailed it to the Enterprise. The "Josh" stories landed him his first writing job on the Enterprise where he adopted his pen name, Mark Twain. So began Twain's literary career. This and other humorous stories of Twain's escapades in the West can be found in *Roughing It*, published in 1871 by Harper and Brothers.

Lucky Boy

Lucky Boy is located on the Lucky Boy pass road near Aurora and four miles south of Hawthorne. It is best visited on a trip to Aurora. If you are coming from Bodie, head north down Bodie Canyon. Thirteen miles out the road forks. If you go right (east) four miles, you'll reach Aurora. If you turn left, you will head north. Several miles from here you will intersect another dirt road. Turn right (east) for several miles to Lucky Boy pass.

From Hawthorne, take Hwy 167 south about six miles. Here a dirt road on your right (west) heads up the mountains to Lucky Boy pass.

In 1906, two stage drivers discovered lead-silver ore on the Bodie-Hawthorne road near Lucky Boy pass summit. The men had been repairing the road after a summer washout. They traced the ore to a ledge six feet from the road. They spent the remainder of the day mining the ore.

The two men worked the Lucky Boy mine off and on for two years and finally traded the mine for a store bill in Hawthorne. The mine was leased to the Chicago Exploration Company in 1908. Other veins were soon found. A stampede resulted in 1909. By 1910, there were 800 in the camp. By 1912, only the successful leasors remained. A new mill was built at the foot of Lucky Boy grade in the 1920's.

The Lucky Boy mine is now being reworked by a small group of men. Steel and machinery have been purchased. No buildings remain from the original camp.

Lucky Boy about 1909. Forbes photo.

Masonic

Masonic is most easily reached from Bridgeport by taking Hwy 182 north five miles. Just before you reach the Bridgeport Lake boat landing, a dirt road on your right leads north 5 miles to Masonic.

Gold was discovered in the summer of 1860 by men who were Masons, hence the name Masonic. The startling Aurora strike of August, 1860 drew interest away from Masonic. The discovery was forgotten for 42 years.

On July 4, 1902, Masonic was rediscovered by John Phillips, Caleb Dorsey and John Bryan. Their claim on the north slope of Masonic Mountain was named the Pittsburg Liberty mine and became the major producer in the district.

In 1904, shafts and tunnels were dug. A vein 3 to 12 feet wide was found. Ore assayed at $35-800 a ton. Some ore assayed at $1,500 a ton. This high grade ore was sacked and shipped for special treatment. In 1904, twenty men were working ten claims. In 1905, other lodes were discovered. By 1907, Masonic was into large scale production. A ten stamp mill and a cyanide plant was built. In 1908, the camp's population was about 500 and a post office was opened. The Chemung mine was discovered in 1909 which was worked until the 1940's.

By 1910, the Pittsburg Liberty had produced $600,000 in gold bullion when the company went bankrupt. By 1911 the camp was nearly deserted and the post office was closed.

Masonic was divided into three sections; Upper, Middle and Lower town.

Lower town was at the north end near the Pittsburg Liberty mine. In Middle Town, on the east side of the gulch, other mines were located: Jump-Up-Joe, Anaconda, Gold Bug, New York, Red Rock, South End and True Friend. Pittsburg Liberty and Jump-Up-Joe were the only bullion producing mines.

In Middle Town, Harvey Boone and Son, Bodie merchants had a store. George Montrose printed the Masonic Pioneer, Masonic's short lived paper, also in Middle Town.

Remains of the Pittsburg Liberty tramway and ruins of a mill and cabins can be seen today.

Upper Town of Masonic in 1904. Wedertz photo, "Mono Diggings"

Stall Brothers Mill in Masonic. Burro happily chomping on sagebrush.
Wedertz photo, "Mono Diggings"

Looking down on Masonic and Mill.

Clinton and Star City

Two silver camps located in Ferris Canyon 14 miles north of Bridgeport, can be reached from Bridgeport two ways: If you're into hiking or horse back riding here is your route: take Hwy 182 and go north 11 miles. One mile south of Devil's Gate, a trail leads off the highway to your left (west). From here to Star City it's about 4 miles, to Clinton 8 miles. About ½ mile down the trail you'll come to a fork. Go to your left. Two and a half miles from there, the trail forks again, go right ½ mile to a dirt road, then left, (west) to Star City.

Two trails leave Star City. Take the trail that heads northwest. Go one mile, the trail will turn north. Go 3 more miles to Clinton.

If you're traveling by car, to reach Clinton and Star City, you must take Hwy 182 north 19 miles to Sweetwater Ranch. Just south of Sweetwater Ranch a dirt road to your left leads 4 miles up Silverado Canyon to Clinton mill site. A trail leads from the mill site 3/4 mile south to Clinton.

Bridgeport at the turn of the century looking west down Main Street. A. A. Forbes.

Inside Courthouse Corner Saloon, Bridgeport. Wedertz, "Mono Diggings"

Typical general store in Bridgeport. Notice wood burning stove in rear.
Wedertz photo, "Mono Diggings"

Dogtown

The earliest gold discovery in Mono County was made at Dogtown, 7 miles south of Bridgeport on Hwy 395. Placer gold was discovered here about 1857 by Cord Norst who later found gold at Monoville to the south. The mounds of dirt created by hydraulic mining are easily seen today on Dogtown Creek, west of 395, just south of the road that leads to Bodie. Look for the California historic marker on the west side of the highway.

The placer gold found in Dogtown Creek had washed down from Dunderberg Mountain where mines were eventually located, among them the Dunder-berg mine. This area came to be known as the Castle Peak Mining District.

It was the Dogtown excitement that attracted men from the western Sierra slope. Several hundred miners worked Dogtown Creek. Crude stone huts and shelters were put up, ruins of some can be seen today. By 1859 the Dogtown excitement had fizzled when gold was discovered at Monoville. (See area map.) The Dogtown diggings were left to the industrious Chinese who worked them for the next ten years. Hydraulic mining was later used at the site. A grave can be found among the ruins and diggings.

Dunderberg mining equipment.

Dunderberg Mine and Mill

Two roads led to the Dunderberg: One can be picked up 2 miles north of Dogtown on the west side of 395. This is a dirt road that leads 6 miles north to the mine.

The easiest route to the mine can be reached at Conway summit. (See area map.) At Conway summit, take the Virginia Creek road and head west 4 miles. Just beyond the pack station, there is a dirt road to your right (north) which leads 3½ miles to the Dunderberg mine and mill site. About a mile and a half down this road you'll come to a fork. Go to your left. The Dunderberg is about 2 miles from the fork.

The Dogtown placer miners followed Dogtown Creek up to Dunderberg Mt. where they discovered the Dunderberg mine. Charles Snyder and Company organized the Castle Peak Mining District July 10, 1867. Snyder sank a 40 foot shaft and hauled the ore to Aurora for milling. The ore assayed $50 a ton in gold and silver.

In 1870, Dr. George Munckton, a Carson City druggist, bought the Dunderberg claims. Exploration tunnels were dug. Ore was found at the 250 ft. level but it assayed poorly. In 1872, having built a 20 stamp mill and a small town, Munckton went bankrupt. The property was sold at a Sheriff's auction in 1872.

In 1878, the property was taken over by A.K. Bryant and G.K. Porter. Water in the mines and high altitude mining brought on failure in 1886. The mill was hauled to Bodie and was known as the Silver Hill mill.

In 1891, English capitalists bought the Dunderberg properties. They re-timbered the tunnels and laid tunnel tracks. By 1903, altitude and water in mines led to the mine's closing. Chlorination and cyanide plants operated at various times.

Charles Snyder, original owner of Dunderberg Mine.

Portion of stamp mill used at the Dunderberg. Wedertz photo

Dunderberg Mill on left, chlorination plant on right. Mine tunnels are located in ridge beyond. Wedertz Photo, "Mono Diggings".

Dunderberg mine, mill, trestle and cabins at turn of century. Wedertz photo, "Mono Diggings"

Monoville

The Monoville ruins are located 1 mile east of Conway Summit in Rattlesnake Gulch. The site can be reached by several routes. The easiest can be picked up on Hwy 395, one mile north of junction 395 and Hwy 167. (See area map.) Another road leads north from Hwy 167, ¼ mile east of the same junction. Taking this road, head east and at the first fork in the road go northwest 2 miles to the diggings. Look for Sinnamon cut, a large opening in the earth caused by hydraulic mining.

Cord Norst discovered gold at Monoville in the spring of 1859. Dick and Lee Vining, for whom the town of Lee Vining was named, were among the first of the Monoville miners. About 150 men win-

tered in Monoville in 1859 and a post office was established in December of that year.

As soon as the Sierra passes cleared in the spring of 1860, men flocked to Monoville. By April, much of the ground around Mono Lake had been staked off. Monoville became the first major settlement east of the Sierra and south of Lake Tahoe.

According to author Frank Wedertz, the gold at Monoville was called "shot gold" by the miners and was "not very coarse but recovered easily in placering." Gold paid $14-15 an ounce. The best claims produced a pound of gold a day; many, though, did not pay as well.

A real problem was enough water for

A Monoville ravine after heavy hydraulic mining.

placering. Though eight creeks flowed into the area during spring run-off, as summer neared and water dwindled, fights broke out over water rights. The lack of water led to an incredible undertaking: the building of two long water ditches. One ditch was dug from the East Walker river 14 miles to Monoville. Two hundred men were hired and worked from June, 1860 to October completing the massive task.

Another ditch was dug from Mill Creek south of Monoville, along the base of the Sierras, north to Monoville.

With water, James Sinnamon applied the hydraulic mining method in Monoville. He washed $70,000 in gold from one area and left a huge gash which is visible today and is know as Sinnamon cut.

Monoville consisted of several hotels and saloons, about 40 houses, some even two story. Timber for building was cut in the Sierras and hauled to Monoville. Mail

James Sinnamon, early Monoville hydraulic miner. Wedertz photo, "Mono Diggings"

The jar on this post contains a recent mining claim in the Monoville area.

came from Genoa, Nevada. At the camp's peak in 1860, Monoville had a population that varied between 500 and 2,000. Unlike other mining camps, Monoville left no history of crime and violence. The post office was closed in April, 1862, due mostly to the Aurora excitement. Some, though, remained behind in Monoville and as late as 1864 the camp was a contestant for Mono County seat.

In 1878, stimulated by the Bodie excitement, both Dogtown and the Monoville diggings were reworked. Louis Lockberg built 1½ miles of sluices at Monoville. The project was taken over in 1881 by John Stewart who reworked the diggings until 1883 when Stewart died.

Because Monoville was the only trading center in the area, it holds an important place in Mono County history. All the major strikes in the area — Bodie, Aurora, Benton and Masonic, were made by men who were supplied provisions at Monoville.

An old car rests among the Monoville ruins.

Lundy

Six miles north of Lee Vining, Mill Creek road junctions at Hwy 395 and 167. Take Mill Creek road and head west five miles to Lundy and Lundy Lake in Mill Creek Canyon.

Lundy was a contemporary and neighbor of Bodie and their fortunes rose and fell together. The Mining camp was named after W. J. Lundy who ran a sawmill in the area and cut lumber for Bodie. Gold was discovered in 1879 and the Homer Mining District was formed.

The district's principal mine was the May Lundy, located high above Lundy on a steep, precarious slope at an elevation of 9500 feet. A tramway was constructed which transported ore 2,000 feet down to the Lundy mill. The Homer Mining District produced 1½ to 3 million dollars, most of which was taken from the May Lundy.

In 1883-84, mining activity slowed at Lundy as in Bodie. There was a crime wave caused by idle hands, booze and frustration. The introduction of cyanide reclamation in 1895 revived the town for a time.

Lundy's newspaper, the Homer Mining Index, was run for a time by Lyin' Jim Townsend, a notorious western journalist whose witty style Mark Twain is said to have imitated. Townsend had worked on a number of mining camp newspapers in Bodie, Virginia City, Pioche and others.

The building of a dam at Lundy Lake has partially submerged part of the old town. Lundy has become quite a tourist attraction because of the area's extraordinary mountain beauty. It's worth a visit, good fishing too.

Lundy about 1906. Forbes photo.

Mill Creek Mining

The lower Mill Creek area was placer and hydraulic mined beginning in 1882 when the Mono Lake Hydraulic Mining Company was formed. Approximately $50,000 was made in washing placers. The small town of Vernon grew up at the base of Copper Mountain west of the 395 and Hwy 167 junction. A small cemetery can be found there. Mill Creek mining ended in 1897.

Mono Mills and Bodie and Benton Railroad

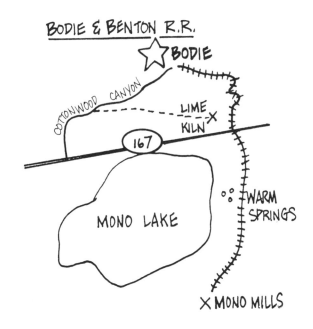

The Mono Mill ruins are located east of Lee Vining near the southeast shore of Mono Lake. The site can be reached by taking Hwy 120 south of Lee Vining and heading east on Hwy 120 for 10 miles. a dirt road on your left (to the North) leads east to the mill ruins.

A large quantity of lumber was needed when Bodie boomed both for building and for shoring up the mines. Squat pinon pines were available in the nearby hills but the wood was inadequate for building and was used instead for fuel. Timber could be had in the Sierras and south of Mono Lake.

In 1881, a group of men formed the Bodie Railway and Lumber Company. Their purpose was to cut timber south of Mono Lake, saw the timber at a mill on the southeast shore, and haul the lumber by train 32 miles to Bodie.

Building of the 3 foot gauge railroad began in early 1881 and was operating by December. The company decided to change its name to the Bodie and Benton Railway and Commercial Company having planned to extend service from Warm Springs on the east shore of Mono Lake, to Benton. By running a line to Benton, the isolated Bodie railroad could connect with the Carson and Colorado Railroad which ran to Carson City and Reno. Though surveyed, the Benton spur was never completed. The Bodie railroad remained an isolated line used only for transporting lumber.

The 32 mile line had two stations: Warm Springs station 5 miles from the mills (named for the three warm springs surrounded by several acres of grassland) and Lime Kiln station 21 ½ miles from the mills and 12 miles from Bodie. (To reach the lime kilns, go to the junction of 395 and Hwy 167, north of Lee Vining. Go east on 167 for about 17 miles. You'll pass an historical marker on your right. A mile or so beyond the marker a dirt road to your left (north) leads three miles northwest to the lime kilns. The pumice sand road is treacherous. Use only a four-wheel drive vehicle, or hike to the site by following the old railroad line.)

Along the 12½ mile stretch from Lime Kiln station to Bodie, there were two switch-backs. One, 6½ miles from Bodie; the other 5 miles from Bodie. There was also a trestle 250 feet long and 50 feet high which crossed a gorge.

The railway consisted of 4 locomotives built in 1880 by the Union Iron Works: The Mono, Inyo, Tybo and the Bodie; three of which, the Mono, Inyo and Tybo were rebuilt 1908-11. There were 30 flat cars, a tank car, five logging cars and a caboose.

The grade from Lime Kiln station to Bodie was steep. Ten or twelve cars would be hauled to Lime Kiln station but from there to Bodie only 3 or 4 cars could be hauled at a time.

The success of the Bodie and Benton Railroad rose and fell with the success and failure of Bodie. In 1915, the Bodie mines declined and many closed. In 1917 the railroad was abandoned and dismantled.

It is possible to trace the old route of the railroad from the Mono Mills across 21 ½ miles of sand flats to the lime kilns. Now and then old bottles, a tie or a spike can be found. It is best to cross the sand flats in a vehicle that can make the trip and will not get stuck in the soft sand. A dune buggy is ideal. Carry plenty of fresh water and fuel for the trip.

Tioga (Bennetville)

Tioga can be reached by taking Hwy 120 from Lee Vining and heading west 10 miles up Tioga Pass. A half mile past Ellery Lake a dirt road to your right (north) leads a half mile to the Tioga historic site.

The Tioga Mine was discovered in 1860 and was known as the Sheepherder mine for many years. In 1878, the Tioga Mining District was formed by the great Sierra Mining Company from Sonora. At considerable expense, Great Sierra built the Tioga road to facilitate transportation of mining machinery. The expense of the road forced Great Sierra into bankruptcy in 1884. No ore was ever milled.

South of Tioga is the Mount Dana Summit mine in Toulumne County, in Yosemite National Park. A cluster of unusual rock houses is located there built and used by miners.

Cabin and mill at Old Mammoth. Los Angeles County Museum.

Old Mammoth City

The well known ski resort of Mammoth Lakes, 45 minutes north of Bishop on Hwy 203, was originally a gold mining camp. Remains of cabins and a mill can be found by taking the main road north toward Lake Mary. Just beyond the Lake Mary entrance, a dirt road to your left leads ½ mile to Old Mammoth.

In 1875, gold was discovered in Mammoth by A. J. Wren and John Briggs. The Alpha claim was discovered in July, 1877, by a prospecting party led by Jim Parker. The boom began in the spring of 1878 and about 20 cabins were soon built. By 1879 the town boasted 6 hotels, 22 saloons, 1 jail, 3 doctors, a school superintendent and a population of 1,000.

In 1878, General George S. Dodge, a Union Pacific railroad contractor, consolidated 5 claims into the "Mammoth Group," which he purchased for $30,000. The Mammoth Mining Company was formed and a 40 stamp mill built powered by water from Lake Mary. Ill fortune plagued the Mammoth Company. By 1880 the company had over-spent $185,000 when it went bankrupt. The company was sold at a Sheriff's auction in 1881.

Pine City and Mineral Park were two lesser camps in the area. Immediate locations are unknown.

Water Wheel powered by water from Lake Mary. Los Angeles County Museum.

Cerro Gordo

Cerro Gordo is located 9 miles east of Keeler, near the top of the Inyo Mountains. To reach Cerro Gordo you must first get to Keeler. If you are approaching from the south on Hwy. 395, at Olancha take Hwy. 190 northeast 10 miles. Hwy 190 will junction with Hwy. 136. Turn left—go north on Hwy. 136 about 3 miles to Keeler. Just before you reach Keeler you will find an historical marker at Cerro Gordo road. Take Cerro Gordo road 9 miles up the mountain to Cerro Gordo. I would suggest making the trip in a smaller car like a VW. Larger cars may have difficulty on the narrow road.

Carson and Colorado depot at Keeler.

Below, Cerro Gordo hotel built in the 1870's.

If approaching from the north on Hwy 395, at Lone Pine, take Hwy 136 southeast 14 miles to Keeler.

The camp of Cerro Gordo is in excellent condition. Today Cerro Gordo is privately owned. You must ask permission to visit the site, but there is usually no objection. When I visited the camp, no one was there and I had the place to myself. It is very important when visiting sites like Cerro Gordo that the public exert extreme courtesy. Theft, destruction of property and littering will prevent others from visiting such sites in the future.

Silver and gold were discovered at Cerro Gordo in 1865 by Pablo Flores. Flores must have been an extremely diligent prospector. It is difficult to imagine anyone hiking to the top of the Inyo Mountains searching for gold. Millions were made by others from Flores' efforts.

In 1866, the Lone Pine Mining District was formed. In 1868, Victor Beaudry, half owner of the Union Mine, built a small

62

furnace. The same year, Mortimer Belshaw and his partners formed the Union Mining Company. They built a smelter and a toll road from Owens Lake.

In 1869, the Owens Lake Silver-Lead Company built a smelter at Swansea, a small settlement several miles north of Keeler on the east shore of Owens Lake. By 1870, Beaudry and Belshaw were producing 9 tons a day.

In 1872, James Bradey, built the Bessie Brady and the Molly Stevens, steamboats which were used to transport ore from Keeler across Owens Lake to Cartago on the west shore. From Cartago, the ore was hauled to San Pedro at a cost of $50 a ton. Keeler in 1883 would become the terminus for the Carson and Colorado Railroad. The Keeler ore, soda and other minerals would then be shipped by rail north to Owenyo where shipments could be trans ferred to the Southern Pacific line and hauled south.

In 1873, Col. Sherman Stevens built a sawmill and flume in nearby Cottonwood Canyon to supply Cerro Gordo with timber and fuel.

In 1874, the Cerro Gordo Water and Mining Company built an 11½ mile pipeline from Miller Springs to Cerro Gordo. The line pumped 90,000 gallons a day. Until this time, 100 burros had been used to haul 6,000 gallons of water per day from Keeler to dry Cerro Gordo.

In 1874, the Union Mine increased its output to 18 tons per day or 400 bars of bullion. The mine made 2 million dollars that year.

But by 1876, Cerro Gordo mines were petering out. Belshaw shut his furnace down. Ore deposits were exhausted in 1877. In 1877, the Union Mine was abandoned.

In 1911, Louis Gordon discovered zinc

Cerro Gordo

ore in the Cerro Gordo mines. Gordon's efforts produced zinc, lead and silver until 1915 when the mines were abandoned. Cerro Gordo mines produced 17 million dollars altogether.

Many buildings remain including a hotel and hoisting works. Remnants of the tramway which transported ore from Cerro Gordo to Keeler are also quite visible. The view of Owens Valley from Cerro Gordo is spectacular. Geologists will appreciate the unique geological formations in the area particularly in regards to shale.

View of Owens Lake from Cerro Gordo.

Laws

Laws is located 4½ miles northeast of Bishop on Silver Canyon Road. Take Hwy. 6 north of Bishop.

On May 20, 1880, the Carson and Colorado Railroad Company was organized by William Sharon, Hume Yerington and Darius Mills. The C and C was to run from Mound House, east of Carson City, south to the Colorado River. The railroad was completed as far as Keeler. The narrow gauge line was used to haul ore from the southern mines, lumber, grain, silver, gold and copper bullion.

Laws was a station on the C and C line and is today a railroad museum. For many years, Laws was simply known as Station. There were so many stations on the line, the depot and settlement were renamed Laws, in honor of R. J. Laws, assistant Superintendent on the line.

In March, 1883, the C and C line was completed as far as Laws. The first train arrived in Laws April 1. By July, the line had reached Keeler.

March, 1900, the C and C line was sold to the Southern Pacific for $2,750,000. R. J. Laws, the hard working superintendent who never missed a day of work, remained as Superintendent. July, 1905, a standard gauge line was run from Mound

House to Tonopah, Nevada, Tonopah then a booming mining camp. Hawthorne was bypassed.

In 1932, passenger service to Laws ended. In 1943, freight service between Mina, Nevada and laws was abandoned and the tracks were removed. The iso- lated line then ran from Laws to Keeler and was the only narrow gauge railroad in operation west of the Rocky Mountains. February, 1959, the Laws depot was closed. On April 30, 1960, locomotive No. 9, made its last trip from Keeler to Laws.

Engine No. 9, now at rest forever.

Laws depot.

Turntable at Laws.

Agent's house at Laws, recently restored.

Chalfant Petroglyphs

The Chalfant Petroglyphs are located 17 miles north of Bishop. They can be reached from Bishop by taking Hwy 6. Once you reach the settlement of Chalfant Valley, the road to the petroglyphs is two miles away. No road sign will point the way to the petroglyphs. The sign was removed by the Bureau of Land Management because portions of the petroglyphs have been destroyed by irresponsible idiots. The petroglyphs are not off limits. The BLM is simply reluctant in giving directions to the site.

Once you are past the Chalfant Valley residences, the second dirt road on your left—to the west, leads ½ mile to the Chalfant Petroglyphs. You will find a posted parking area at the end of this road.

The Chalfant Petroglyphs were made by ancient Indians on a cliff along a branch of the Owens River. The petroglyph site was obviously an Indian encampment located in a cove beneath limestone cliffs. The limestone is quite soft and easily carved upon. Indians with nothing better to do, could have easily carved the figures on the cliffs above their camp. The Chalfant Petroglyphs are really worth a visit. Wonderful exploring an area where ancient peoples lived thousands of years ago.

About The Author

For the past ten years George Williams III has traveled throughout California and Nevada researching and writing about the legends, outlaws, boom towns and fast women of the early days. Since the publication of his first book, ROSA MAY: THE SEARCH FOR A MINING CAMP LEGEND, in 1980, he has earned a reputation as a detailed researcher and a writer whose books take the reader along with him on his back road travels. 1981, Williams published THE GUIDE TO BODIE AND EASTERN SIERRA HISTORIC SITES, reprinted six times in four years. In 1984 he published three new books, THE MURDERS AT CONVICT LAKE, THE REDLIGHT LADIES OF VIRGINIA CITY, NEVADA and THE SONGWRITER'S DEMO MANUAL AND SUCCESS GUIDE.

In 1981 Williams was nominated for the prestigious Commonwealth Club of California Literary Award for ROSA MAY. In 1984 he was nominated for the Nobel Prize in Literature for the same book.

Williams lives with his wife Edie and their two children, Sarah and Michael, in Riverside, California. During the summers, he and his family travel the West in search of true stories to write about. Williams is now at work on several books. Williams frequently speaks at colleges, highschools and clubs about early California and Nevada history, writing and publishing and the music business. Those who wish to contact the author about speaking engagements may contact him through this publisher.

Tree By The River Publishing
Box 413-S
Riverside, CA 92502

Acknowledgements

As always, I thank my wife, Edie, for her encouragement and personal sacrifice during the time this book was written. Edie also caught many manuscript errors and proofread the manuscript and typeset.

I am especially in debt to several people for their generosity: Author Frank S. Wedertz allowed me to use several of his photos which appear in *Bodie: 1859-1900* and *Mono Diggings*. Tod Watkins and Russ Johnson at Chalfant Press supplied photo copies of the Wedertz Photos.

Bill Mason and John Cahoon of the Los Angeles Museum of Natural History were a big help during research. Bill Mason was especially helpful in obtaining the A. A. Forbes photos.

I am in debt to A. A. Forbes and Burton Frasher, Sr., who took many of the photos.

I thank the following folks who were born and raised in Bodie who shared their memories with me: Mrs. Bell, Bob Bell, "Slick" Bryant, Stuart and Sadie Cain, Richie Conway, Herb Dechambeau, Helen Evans, Bill Glenn, Anna McKenzie, Warren Loose, Guy McInnis, and Charles Ah Yuen Kee.

I would also like to thank Penny Williams and Dorrie Livoni of Graphica in Riverside for their typesetting and graphic art help. Their professionalism and speed made putting this book together a lot easier than it would have been.

And last but always first: I thank Jesus Christ for caring about me when I didn't care about Him, for making the wrong in my life right, for giving me my wife, Edie, and my children and my work. Thank you, thank you.

Bibliography

In regards to the Bodie history included in this book: I made a real effort not to re-hash what previous authors have written on the subject. This was not entirely possible. One must deal with facts. More extensive Bodie histories are available for the serious history enthusiast. I suggest these books:

Bodie: 1859-1900, by Frank S. Wedertz, is the most thorough history of Bodie, based on ten years of research. This book is well documented and Wedertz has gathered a fine collection of photos.

Bodie Bonanza, by Warren Loose, covers Bodie's boom years extensively; is well documented with lots of photos.

The Ghost Town of Bodie, by Russ and Anne Johnson, approaches Bodie's history as reported in the newspapers of the day. Plenty of photos.

Mining Camp Days, by Emil Billeb, covers the latter years of Bodie's history, after 1900. Many photos. Railroad buffs will enjoy the photos of the Bodie and Benton railroad locomotives.

I found the following books quite helpful during research:

Ashbaugh, Don: *Nevada's Turbulent Yesterday*, Westernlore Press, 1963

Bancroft, Hubert: *California Inter Pocula*, The History Co., 1890

Browne, J. Ross: *Mining Adventures*, Paisano Press, reprint, 1961.

Cain, Ella: *The Story of Bodie*, Fearon Publishers, 1956.

Chalfant, W.A.:   *Guns, Gold and Ghost Towns*, Stanford University Press.

Elliot, Russell R: *History of Nevada*, University of Nebraska Press, 1973.

Hulse, James W: *The Nevada Adventure*, University of Nevada Press, 1965.

Miller, Don: *Ghost Towns of California*, Pruett Publishing.

Paher, Stanley W: *Nevada Ghost Towns and Mining Camps*, Howell-North Books.

Smith, Grant: *"Bodie: Last of the Old-Time Mining Camps."*

Twain, Mark: *Roughing It*, Harper and Brothers, 1871.

Wasson, Joseph: *Bodie and Esmeralda*, Spaulding, Bento and Co.

Wedertz, Frank: *Mono Diggings*, Sierra Media, 1978.

Williams, George, III: *Rosa May: The Search For A Mining Camp Legend*, Tree By The River Publishing, 1980.

Eastern Sierra Business Directory

The following is a collection of Eastern Sierra Businesses. You will find motels, sport shops, restaurants, museums, liquor stores, reservation services and realtors here. All are here to meet your needs in the Eastern Sierra. I sincerely urge you to give these businesses a call when you need their type of service.

Sincerely,

George Williams III

Big Pine   Bishop

72

Help Save Mono Lake Today!

Mono Lake, at the foot of the Eastern Sierra near Yosemite National Park, needs your help NOW! This mysterious and beautiful lake is the home for thousands of migratory birds. Over 95% of all California Gulls nest on Mono Lake's two islands.

Since 1947, Los Angeles has diverted the streams which fill Mono Lake into its own aqueduct. This has caused the lake to drop in level and has threatened this wonderful nesting place.

You can help save Mono Lake by visiting the Mono Lake Committee in Lee Vining. These people are working hard to save **your** lake. They can use your moral support, prayers, and most of all, **money**, which is needed to protect Mono Lake in our courts system.

Please help me save Mono Lake today by sending a tax deductible gift to: **Mono Lake Committee, PO Box 29, Lee Vining, CA 93541.** I support the Mono Lake Committee. Won't you?

Thank you. *George Williams III*

PROSTITUTION

ROSA MAY: THE SEARCH FOR A MINING CAMP LEGEND Virginia City, Carson City and Bodie California were towns Rosa May worked as a prostitute and madam between 1873-1912. Read her remarkable true story based on 3 1/2 years of intensive research. Includes 30 rare photos and 26 personal letters of Rosa May's recently discovered. 240 pages. **AUTOGRAPHED BY THE AUTHOR.** Soft cover quality, $9.95; hard cover, gold embossed, $16.95. Soon to be a television movie.

"Both stories—Rosa May's and the author's—are told in a rich, deeply personal and yet scholarly work of regional history."
Los Angeles Times Book Review.

THE REDLIGHT LADIES OF VIRGINIA CITY, NEVADA Virginia City, Nevada near Reno was the richest mining camp in the American West. The silver from its mines built San Francisco and helped the Union win the Civil War. The town prospered from 1860-1895. The town had one of the largest redlight districts in America. Virginia City's wealth attracted women from all parts of the world. Author Williams tells of the strange lives of the redlight girls, of their legends and violent deaths. Here is the true story of madam Jessie Lester, shot by her lover yet refused to give police his name. And Julia Bulette, the highly respected prostitute who was violently murdered in her bed. Based on newspaper accounts, county records and U.S. Census materials. Perhaps the most informative book on American prostitution in the old West. Many rare, historic photos of prostitutes, madams, pimps. Includes historic letters by prostitues, madams, lovers and other historic documents. **AUTOGRAPHED BY THE AUTHOR.** Quality soft cover, $5.95; hard cover, gold embossed $12.95.

"Rare photos, maps and letters from prostitutes, madams and lovers spark this treatise on the world's oldest profession as practiced in the richest mining town in the West in the late nineteenth century."
True West

GHOST TOWNS

THE GUIDE TO BODIE AND EASTERN SIERA HISTORIC SITES True story of the rise and fall of Bodie—California's most famous gold mining town, today a ghost town, California State Park and National Historic Site. Once known as the most violent mining town in the West, murders were a daily occurence in this mountain town wher millions were made in a few years. A beautiful full color cover with over 100 rare, historic photos. 88 pages. Quality soft cover, $9.95; hard cover, gold embossed, $18.95.

"A fine account of the rise and fall of Bodie—one of the West's most famous gold mining towns."
Pasadena Star News

OUTLAWS

THE MURDERS AT CONVICT LAKE True story of the infamous 1871 Nevada State Penitentiary break in which 29 outlaws—murderers, rapists, train robbers—escaped. Six convicts fled more than 200 miles into Mono and Inyo counties California in the Eastern Sierra. They pledged to kill anyone who got in their way. Near Bridgeport they killed a young Pony Express rider, Billy Poor. In a terrible shootout at Monte Diablo, today known as Convict lake near Mammoth Lakes ski resort, the convicts killed two men. They fled south to Bishop where they werd captured, tried and two convicts were hanged. Here is the intense true story based on newspaper accounts of the day and public records. 18 rare, historic photos and dramatic scene depictions by Dave Comstock, well known artist and author. **AUTOGRAPHED BY THE AUTHOR.** Quality soft cover, $4.95; hard cover, gold embossed, $12.95.

"...rich in both text and pictures. As always, Williams captures the flavor of his subject in great detail, while capturing the reader's interest...a must for anyone wishing to know more about our rich history."
Buddy Noonan, The Review, Mammoth Lakes

New Mark Twain in the West Series!
Critically acclaimed by Mark Twain historians and fans.
Based on recently discovered letters and journals, four new books reveal intimate details of Mark Twain's life in

California and Nevada.

MARK TWAIN IN NEVADA AND CALIFORNIA

MARK TWAIN: HIS ADVENTURES AT AURORA AND MONO LAKE When Sam Clemens arrived in Nevada, August, 1861, he hoped to strike it rich in the silver mines. For six months he tried prospecting and silver mining at Aurora, Nevada, near Bodie, California. Clemens didn't strike it rich but his hard luck mining days led to his writing career. Based on Mark Twain's own letters, this book gives readers the firsthand account of Clemens' life as a struggling miner. Points out places, like Mono Lake, where Mark Twain camped, fished and hiked, places you can visit today. Over 60 rare, historic photos, some published here for the first time. 100 pages. **AUTOGRAPHED BY THE AUTHOR.** Quality soft cover, $6.95; hard cover, gold embossed, $12.95.
"Williams has thoroughly covered an important aspect of Mark Twain's life as a silver miner."
    Bill Dalton, Historian and Publisher

MARK TWAIN: HIS LIFE IN VIRGINIA CITY, NEVADA Having failed to strike it rich at Aurora and gone broke, Clemens is offered a reporting job by the *Territorial Enterprise* in Virginia City. At first reluctant to give up his mining endeavors, Clemens relents and takes the job. He walks more than 130 miles to Virginia City across the Nevada desert. Arriving in mid-October, Clemens begins a twenty-one month stint as local reporter, a job which permanently change his life. Here Clemens adopted Mark Twain as his pen name and won notoriety as a humorist and character. Williams shows us the young Mark Twain was a fun loving hell raiser who drank too much, invented horrible murder stories and fled town after threatening a rival editor to duel. Williams also gives the true account of how Clemens really got his name, "Mark Twain." Revealed for the first time in this account. **AUTOGRAPHED BY THE AUTHOR.** 208 pages. 60 rare, historical photographs. Quality soft cover, $9.95; hard cover, gold embossed, $24.95.
"...provides much information about the Territorial Enterprise, and Twain's associates on the paper..One useful section provides current maps and instructions for visiting the sites of Twain's days in Nevada."
    Kirkus Reviews

NEW FOR 1988! **MARK TWAIN: JACKASS HILL AND THE JUMPING FROG** In May, 1864, Mark Twain leaves Virginia City for San Francisco. At first Twain reports for the San Francisco *Call*. Finding the editor and the work repressive, Twain begins his associations with Bret Harte and other well known West Coast writers. Twain begins a successful career as a free lance writer contributing to the *Golden Era* and *the Californian*. After a dispute with police, Twain leaves for Jim Gillis' Jackass Hill cabin near Sonora. Here Twain stays for three months, learns about pocket gold mining and discovers the "Jumping Frog of Calaveras County, " story. This story, published in 1865, creates instant national success for Twain. Many rare, historic photos. **AUTOGRAPHED BY THE AUTHOR.** Quality soft cover, $5.95; hard cover, gold embossed, $12.95.
"Williams for the first time shows how important Mark Twain's three month stay on Jackass Hill was to his first literary success. Much funny and useful information here."
    Riverside Press-Enterprise

NEW FOR 1988! **ON THE ROAD WITH MARK TWAIN IN CALIFORNIA AND NEVADA** Here is a wonderful travel guide to places where Mark Twain lived, wrote, mined, lectured and camped while living in California and Nevada, 1861-68. Williams tells what Twain was doing at each historic site. This is a book for the traveler who wishes to visit Twain's historic haunts and is looking for general information about Twain's life in California and Nevada. Includes useful road maps and road directions to all historic sites. Many historic photographs and photos of historic sites as they look today. **AUTOGRAPHED BY THE AUTHOR.** Quality soft cover, $9.95; hard cover, gold embossed, $16.95.
"When it comes to writing useful travel guides, Williams is a champ. This useful book is intersting and plain fun. Every Twain fan should have this book."
    Bill Dalton, Historian and Publisher

HOT SPRINGS OF THE EASTERN SIERRA. Here are listed more than 40 hot springs between California's Owens Valley, north along Highway 395 through the Eastern Sierra recreation corrdior to Gerlach , Nevada. The author has tracked down every hot spring worth soaking in. Included are such popular places as Hot Creek, near Mammoth Lakes and many hot springs only known to locals. The author gives easy to follow road directions to each hot spring, provides camping details and his "2 cents," about each spring. You'll have a great time discovering these wonderful places. **AUTOGRAPHED BY THE AUTHOR.** 72 pages. $6.95 pap., $12.95 hard cover.

And on the Music Business:

The Songwriter's Demo Manual and Success Guide shows the songwriter and aspiring group how to make a professional "demo," demonstration tape, at home or in the recording studio. The quality of a demo tape greatly determines whether or not a song is published or a group lands a recording contract. George Williams, a published songwriter, recording studio owner and producer, covers the complete demo process: choosing the songs, rehearsing, arranging, finding an inexcpensive recording studio, how to get free recording time and many more money saving tips. Once the demo is recorded, it must be placed into the hands of the right people. Williams explains how the music business operates, who the important people are, how to make contact with them and how to sell your songs in person and by mail. 200 pages, many photos. $12.95, soft cover, 24.95, hard cover gold embossed. **AUTOGRAPHED BY THE AUTHOR.**
"A valuable, well organized handbook and a cogent look at a tough show-business field...just may be the most helpful guide of its kind...could provide gifted novices with the ticket for success."
    Booklist

Order Form
All mail orders are mailed the day we receive your order by bookrate postage.

Name_____Address_____
City_____State_____Zip_____

Please send me the following:
__Copy(ies) ROSA MAY__pap. $9.95__hard cover $18.95
__Copy(ies) GUIDE TO BODIE __pap.9.95--hard cover $18.95
__Copy(ies) MURDERS AT CONVICT LAKE__pap.$4.95__hard cover $12.95
__Copy(ies) REDLIGHT LADIES OF VIRGINIA CITY __pap.$5.95__hard cover $12.95
__Copy(ies) MARK TWAIN: HIS ADVENTURES AT AURORA__pap $6.95__hard cover
    $12.95
__Copy(ies) MARK TWAIN: HIS LIFE IN VIRGINIA CITY _pap. $9.95 __hard cover $24.95
__Copy(ies) MARK TWAIN: JACKASS HILL AND THE JUMPING FROG __pap.
    $5.95__hard $10.95
__Copy(ies) ON THE ROAD WITH MARK TWAIN IN CALIFORNIA AND NEVADA,
  __pap. $9.95 __hard cover $18.95
__Copy(ies) HOT SPRINGS OF THE EASTERN SIERRA __pap. $6.95__hard cover $12.95

Total for books $_____
Add $1.50 postage for 1st book, .50 for each additional
Total enclosed $_____

THANK YOU FOR YOUR MAIL ORDER !
Send check or money order to: Tree By The River Publishing, Box 935, Dayton, Nevada